FINDING JOY WHEN LIFE IS HARD

Life is often hard, but the Book of Philippians shows us that we can find Joy in life

Compiled & Written By
Ronald Parrs

Copyright Information

Contents

Finding Joy: the Book of Philippians - Overview

Introduction - Who the Philippians were and why Paul sought them out.

Week 1 - Prayer First. Philippians 1:1-11. Praying should be our first action before really taking action. And we should not only be praying for the activity and its success, we should be praying the all of the people involved. That's how Paul begins this great book of Joy.

Week 2 - Homesick. Philippians 1:12-30. Home is where the heart is. Home is place that, when we get there, we know that it's home. But we are all here. We Christians have a divine work to do. Let's garner some perspective of this passage.

Week 3 - Attitude Adjustment. Philippians 2:1-11. Jesus is our model for living. It is God's intention that all of His children become Christlike. As we adjust our attitude we are able to better imitate Him and become part of the reconciliation process between God and mankind.

An Aside - The Deity of Jesus Christ. Philippians 2:6-11. One of the most important Doctrines of the Christian faith that we must have a firm grasp of is that of the Deity of Christ. Jesus' complete divinity and complete humanity is essential to understanding our salvation and eternal life.

Week 4 - Shining Examples. Philippians 2:12-18. What does it mean to "shine"? And furthermore, why does God want us to shine in the first place? Let's find some answers to those questions.

Week 5 - A Couple of Good Friends. Philippians 2:19-30. God is a God of relationships. We are not meant to go it alone. Paul writes about 2 very important men, and friends, who labored with him in the preaching of the Gospel. We need friends.

Week 6 - the Right Credentials. Philippians 3:1-11. All of us like to have others know who we are. We love titles and the credentials that go along with them. The problem though is that those credentials are meaningless in God's economy. Let's find out what's really important.

Week 7 - Pressing On. Philippians 3:12-4:1. We all live as part of a journey in life. There are mountains and valleys. We press on toward our eternal goal, Heaven. Heaven is not necessarily the world's goal. What is your goal?

Week 8 - Anxiety, Depression & Restoration. Philippians 4:2-9. How we interact with one another can determine our state of mind and more importantly, how we interact with God Himself. God want us whole and He provides all that we need.

Week 9 - Anxiety, Depression & Restoration; Part 2. The path to restoration does not have to be long or arduous. The Holy Spirit, writing through Paul in the Epistle to the Colossians (immediately following Philippians), provides what we need.

Week 10 - Regular Maintenance. Philippians 4:8-9 is one of those verses that each of us should have memorized. It's a kind of checklist as we are transformed especially in the mind.

Week 11 - Strong Enough. We say that we're "content" in all things or that we're "strong enough", but is that really true or are we acting "pious"? Paul's state of contentedness and strength is a high standard that very few of us actually come close to achieving; but then again, all things are possible... Philippians 4:10-23.

Week 12 - Therefore... What's the "therefore" there for? Let's recap.

Final Thoughts of Joy – Wrapping up with several concluding thoughts of how to find Joy

Appendix – Study Leader's Notes

Finding Joy: the Book of Philippians

The Apostle Paul's letter to the Philippian church is often referred to as the Bible's book of "Joy".

Philippians has received that moniker because the word "joy" (or its forms) is mentioned sixteen times through its four short chapters.

What I like about reading the Book to the Philippians is that you can sit down and read it in under thirty minutes (even if you're a slow reader like me). Philippians is a simple book with lessons about life, and in particular, how to live our Christian lives in a way that is not only honoring to Jesus, but also to one another - as brothers and sisters in Christ.

It's also a book of life lessons as we navigate the world around us. And not just the world, but more importantly, the PEOPLE who don't know the Good News of the Gospel of Jesus Christ that intersect our lives day in and day out.

Philippians is a simple book, but it teaches great doctrines of our Christian faith. These are Doctrines that we are to understand as we proclaim our faith to friends, relatives, co-workers, and everyone that we come into contact with. We are to become Christ-like as we trod this earth, waiting for our heavenly reward and our reunion with our Savior and our God.

Let's take a walk for the next 14 weeks or so and see what Paul, inspired by the Holy Spirit, will teach us.

Finding Joy: Introduction

So what's so special about the Book of Philippians or the city of Philippi?

Good questions. Understanding a little bit about the city of Philippi and its people helps us to understand Paul's letter. Whenever we understand the surrounding context, many things become clearer. For example, a quick browse of the letter reveals that there are no Old Testament quotes. Why?

Furthermore, why did Paul even venture to Philippi in the first place? Understanding the city answers the first question. Divine Providence and guidance answer the second.

Let's answer the second question first.

Paul went to Philippi because of a dream. While on his second missionary journey through Asia Minor, Paul had a dream one night to travel to the region of northern Greece, better known as Macedonia. Macedonia is Macedonia and Greece is Greece, even today. Never call a Macedonian a Greek if you know what's good for you! They may share some similarities, but they are Macedonians nonetheless. Now, back to the why.

We read in Acts 16:6-10, [6] *And they* [Paul and his ministry companions] *went through the*
region of Phrygia and Galatia, having been forbidden by the Holy Spirit to speak the word in
Asia. [7] *And when they had come up to Mysia, they attempted to go into Bithynia, but the*
Spirit of Jesus did not allow them. [8] *So, passing by Mysia, they went down to Troas.* [9] *And a*
vision appeared to Paul in the night: a man of Macedonia was standing there, urging him
and saying, "Come over to Macedonia and help us." [10] *And when Paul had seen the vision,*
immediately we sought to go on into Macedonia, concluding that God had called us to
preach the gospel to them.

And so Paul and his friends, including Dr. Luke, traveled from Asia Minor to Macedonia. The first major city they would reach would be Philippi. Philippi was named for Philip II of Macedonia, the father of Alexander the Great. Its importance lay in its location on the great

Via Egnatia, the main road connecting the eastern parts of the empire with Rome. The fact that this was also a Roman colony meant its citizens were Roman citizens, with every Roman privilege. We remember that Paul used his Roman citizenship as his "ace" when seeking justice.

Philippi had a large population of retired Roman military officers and their families, who mingled with the locals. There were few Jews, so there was no synagogue (and that was the reason for not quoting the Old Testament). Philippians would be a true first stop toward reaching the Gentiles. These were people who had little or no knowledge of the God of Israel. Paul and his friends would be breaking completely unplowed ground, sharing the Gospel of Christ. Let's face it, these folks were heathens. They were unchurched. Sounds like what many of us have to contend with regularly, as God has us "in the world," doesn't it?

Paul, following God's lead, had first gone to His people, the Jews. Some accepted the Word; some did not. God's chosen people completely rejected His Word. Now, Paul would continue to follow God's lead into the Gentile world.

Paul, Silas, and his friends would share the Gospel and then teach some completely foreign concepts to the Macedonians. Instead of heading for the synagogue to reason with the local Jews, they would head out to find a place to pray and see who God would bring to them.

And that's what living the Christian life is all about, isn't it? Being with God (through prayer and personal worship) and being open to His direction for our lives, living and following His plan. When we make His plan our plan, God does amazing things.

Some things were easy, some not so easy. Preaching was easy. Being stripped, beaten, and thrown into the local jail for inciting a riot was not. But God still had a reason. The jailer and his household would be saved and baptized after God rocked the area with an earthquake, as we read in Acts 16:16-40.

In Philippi, God demonstrates His love, care, and respect for women by bringing Lydia, a prominent local businesswoman, to Himself. God would use her to be the apparent center of this new body of believers. She had the means to provide for Paul and many others, but almost more importantly, Lydia had the influence. As Lydia came to a saving knowledge of Jesus Christ, God would provide her with a testimony of her personal salvation. Many people in Philippi and the surrounding environs would hear the Gospel and come to Christ.

As an aside, Christianity, more than any other religious system, includes women and elevates them to prominent positions within His Plan. God's plan includes women as well as men. Only when we men abdicate our responsibilities as leaders of our households, communities, and even churches, will God raise up women to lead. Like men, women have been created in God's image. Women are as much a part of the dynamic of the Kingdom as men. We must not forget that.

So what about Philippi? It may have been a Roman colony; it wasn't considered a backwards or backwater town; it was an average city of the empire. And yet it was a "crossroads" city where new believers and pre-believers came and went. The Way was going to spread into the Roman Empire and beyond. And still, Philippi was an ordinary first-century AD (or CE, as some now put it) city, made up of ordinary people leading ordinary lives. They struggled with the same issues we do today, maybe just not as complicated. But the same nonetheless. They quarreled, boasted about their favorite preacher, and even dealt with ego. Some people even had anxiety issues. Coming together as a local body of believers, a church, they would do their best - and sometimes fail - to lead a good Christian life. It would be hard at times, but God would provide. And in turn, the Philippian believers would help provide for their brothers and sisters in other churches and for Paul himself.

This little book of Philippians, which only takes about 30 minutes to read, is not just for people of long ago; it is for us, living today in the early twenty-first century. The Bible is always relevant because it is God's letter of love, hope, and joy to His people wherever - and whenever - they may live.

When it all comes down to it, it's all about God seeking out His creation, His people, isn't it? Since the Fall in the Garden, God has been seeking out men and women to save us from ourselves and our inherent, life-smothering sin. God desires fellowship with us. God wants us, all of us, to turn to Him and accept His free gift of eternal life through the shed blood of Jesus Christ, His Son.

One of the great joys of being a believer in the finished work of Christ, a Christian, is that we do have joy. We can rejoice in God our Savior. We can rejoice that we didn't have to do anything to merit eternal life except to believe and accept Jesus' atoning work at the Cross as payment for our individual sins. One day, we will experience true joy as we see Jesus face-to-face.

Philippians and Joy. They go together, don't they?

Yes, they do.

Finding Joy: Pray First

So, you've been given a new task or provided an opportunity that is literally life changing.

And it's not only life-changing for you, but for countless others that will either come after you or be influenced by you - directly or indirectly. What do you do? Take your marching orders or instructions and start?

I can tell you that I've done exactly that. What follows doesn't seem right. The task or the opportunity doesn't come together as I thought it would. You know what I am referring to. Something similar has happened to you, too. Why?

The instructions were simple. You had the right goals, the right people; all the "stuff" that would make it a success, but it doesn't come together. Then it finally dawns on me...

Did I remember to pray first?

Ouch! That hurt.

But that simple act of pausing to pray could have made all the difference between success and failure, or marginal success and phenomenal success.

As the Apostle Paul begins his letter to the Philippian church, he encourages them. But it's not the kind of encouragement that we usually give. You know, "go out there and win!" or some such thing. Instead, Paul simply writes,

[3] I thank my God in all my remembrance of you, [4] always in every prayer of mine for you all making my prayer with joy, [5] because of your partnership in the gospel from the first day until now. [6] And I am sure of this, that he who began a good work in you will bring it to completion at the day of Jesus Christ. [7] It is right for me to feel this way about you all, because I hold you in my heart, for you are all partakers with me of grace, both in my imprisonment and in the defense and confirmation of the gospel. [8] For God is my witness, how I yearn for you all with the affection of Christ Jesus. [9] And it is my prayer that your love

may abound more and more, with knowledge and all discernment, [10]so that you may approve what is excellent, and so be pure and blameless for the day of Christ, [11]filled with the fruit of righteousness that comes through Jesus Christ, to the glory and praise of God. Philippians 1:3-11.

Paul begins his letter to the church in Philippi with a simple prayer.

Although Paul didn't spend too much time in Philippi, his time spent there was necessary to the fulfillment of God's plan for the proclamation of the Gospel to the world.

As we learned in the Introduction to this series, Philippi may not have been the largest city in Macedonia. Still, it was important as a gateway or crossroads city sitting on the Via Egnatia at the eastern end of the Macedonian territory before going east into Asia Minor. By the same token, for anyone traveling west toward Rome from the eastern provinces (particularly by land), you would have passed through Philippi.

Philippi was not a Jewish enclave. There was no synagogue. Paul was squarely in Gentile territory. He, Silas, and the rest of his band of evangelists would be preaching to completely unchurched people. These folks had no working knowledge of the Law of Moses. Monotheism was just one of the "new" and "crazy" sects (there were probably even rumors that they needed to clarify; see verses 15-18; we'll discuss that in a later lesson). But Paul had much in common with these people: they were lost sinners in need of a Savior who needed to hear the Gospel and experience true liberation and salvation. That was Paul's mission.

Teaching these new believers about God and the finished work of Jesus Christ was one thing; teaching them how to live a completely different lifestyle with a completely different focus would be another. He would need to teach them the basics. And one of those basics is the discipline of simple, yet effective prayer.

Paul had firsthand experience of the importance of prayer. He knew what prayer could do. He knew what prayer did do. And now, by example in a letter, he would reinforce - and even teach - this most effective discipline of the Christian way of life.

Praying Purposefully.

As we look at these opening verses of Philippians and this simple prayer, we learn how to pray for others in our spheres of influence. There are three purposes to praying (interceding) for others. When we pray for others, whether they know it or not, we pray to Encourage, to Instruct or Teach, and to Remind.

Let's go through Paul's prayer and understand these purposes.

Praying in order to Encourage. Virtually the entire passage of Philippians 1:3-11 is full of encouragement. Look at what Paul says to them: *"I thank my God* [for] *you...", "making my prayer with joy...", "I hold you in my heart...", how I yearn for you all with the affection of Christ Jesus."* Paul's focus is on the Philippian believers lives. He uses the word "you" over and over again.

These are very personal words, rich with meaning, and although the letter is written to the entire church, it can be read as a letter written specifically to you or me.

I don't know about you, but I can't tell you how encouraged I am to know that many people, perhaps even you, are praying for my family and me in this way. Your words - your prayers - are an encouragement to me to continue moving forward even though it may be difficult.

Every one of us needs to receive a letter like this from time to time. Over the years, people have come up to me quietly and personally to say similar things. They are honestly interested in how I'm doing and what I'm doing. They may not know every detail of my struggle, but their words are a tremendous encouragement to continue pressing forward. And that's exactly what the Philippian Christians needed.

Praying to Instruct. Yes instruct. When we are praying in silence or in our respective prayer closets, it may seem difficult, but we can still pray to instruct or teach. And as Paul writes this prayer out, he can teach them about living the Christian life. How does that work? Good question. Here's what I've come to understand.

As others pray for me and my needs, they also pray that I am in God's Will and Plan. As I pray for others, I am praying that they would be in God's Will and Plan as well.

As we go through the process of living, as we go through the process of changing our (my) plan for life over to God's Plan, we (I) learn. When we say that the *" prayer of a righteous person has great power as it is working."*, James 5:16, what are we really saying? I believe that means that God will use that prayer to effective move in a person or a situation.

God always has us learning new lessons about life and living, about His Kingdom versus this temporary earthly history. Teaching is a process. We go from simple understanding to apprehending or grasping (firmly holding onto something).

In these short verses, what is Paul teaching the Philippians? How about "confidence", verse 6, confidence that *"that he who began a good work in you will carry it on to completion until the day of Jesus Christ."* They hadn't seen, or until then, even heard of Jesus or His teaching, never mind His death and life-restoring resurrection. These Philippians had to have confidence in the complete unknown. They would have to trust and have faith. Furthermore, this *"good work"* was just the beginning. God would carry it - whatever the work would happen to be, it's different for each of us - through to completion; that also means that it's God's timing, not ours.

The Philippians, and even all of us today, were taught and therefore learned that we are works in progress. God's work is always ongoing.

Paul also taught them about grace. He not only taught them, but he also demonstrated God's grace; the grace that brings the unbeliever to the Cross. Paul's prayer and teaching were that they would be able to defend and confirm the Gospel of Christ (verse 7). Paul was an apologetics guy. He knew, and I'm sure he taught, the Philippians how to reason with other unbelievers.

Finally, in teaching, Paul emphasized the necessity of discernment (verses 9 and 10). That's something we all need. Every Christian must be able to not only confirm and defend the Gospel, but also discern God's Truth from the lies of the unbelieving world around them. How important is that, especially today?

Praying to Remind. In a way, we've touched on this while looking at Encouraging, Instructing, or Teaching. But it's good to be reminded! We all need to be reminded - and some of us more so than others.

What did Paul remind them of as he prayed? Paul reminded them of how much they were thought of. I don't know about you, but I like to be reminded that someone, especially far away, is thinking about me and praying for my well-being. Not only is that comforting, but it is also humbling. Paul, in a similar fashion, reminded them of the importance of love toward one another and toward God. The "affection of Jesus Christ" is a two-way street. He loves each of us so much just for who and Whose we are, and we are to love Him in return just for Who He is.

Paul also reminded the Philippians to be - to live - pure and blameless lives. Oh, how often is that difficult to do! The unbelieving world around us always has its eyes on us believers in Jesus. The unbeliever listens to every word we speak and watches our actions. They do this not necessarily to trip us up, though some do, but more often to see if we are "real". They want what we have only if it's real. Our world, as plastic as it is, wants not only to believe in something, but to have and hold something eternal and solid; they are tired of fakes and forgeries. We are to rightly reflect the love and life that only God can provide through the finished work of Jesus. We are to even remind our unsaved friends and relatives Whose we are, in a loving and real way.

Jesus' work may be finished, but His work in and through us is not.

"[H]e who began a good work in you will carry it on to completion until the day of Jesus Christ." We need to be reminded of that. No, we're not perfect - none of us. Not a single one. And you know what? That's really okay with me. I am, you are, a magnificent work in progress!

An interesting thing to note. Prayer is an amazing thing. Although we are praying for others outwardly, the Holy Spirit often works in us. Think of the times when you've prayed that a family member or sibling in Christ be encouraged as they go through a trial, were you encouraged as well? How about when you prayed that the co-worker who's always bumbling and stumbling through their day would learn to do their job well? As you prayed for them, how did the Holy Spirit begin to instruct you to possibly do your job in a better, more effective way? Finally, and this hits home for me, when I've prayed that others remember or are reminded of certain things (personal, professional, spiritual), the Holy Spirit taps me on the shoulder to remind me of my obligations.

Prayer is rarely unidirectional, except when we are in praise and thanksgiving to Him Who is worthy of that adoration. Much of prayer time and life ends up being bi-directional: me to God and God to me. It can also be omnidirectional as God answers our prayers for ourselves, our families, our brothers and sisters in Christ, our unsaved friends, family, and acquaintances, and frankly, the world at large. God's abounding love for His creation is without measure and even understanding.

The Philippians then, like us today, are also reminded to love. Love God. Love one another. Grace and love, true grace and love, are what separate (at least should) Christians from everyone else. The Apostle John fleshes this entire idea out well in 1 John 4:7-21.

7 Beloved, let us love one another, for love is from God, and whoever loves has been born of
God and knows God. 8 Anyone who does not love does not know God, because God is love.
9 In this the love of God was made manifest among us, that God sent his only Son into the
world, so that we might live through him. 10 In this is love, not that we have loved God but
that he loved us and sent his Son to be the propitiation for our sins. 11 Beloved, if God so

loved us, we also ought to love one another. [12] No one has ever seen God; if we love one another, God abides in us and his love is perfected in us.

[13] By this we know that we abide in him and he in us, because he has given us of his Spirit.
[14] And we have seen and testify that the Father has sent his Son to be the Savior of the
world. [15] Whoever confesses that Jesus is the Son of God, God abides in him, and he in God.
[16] So we have come to know and to believe the love that God has for us. God is love, and
whoever abides in love abides in God, and God abides in him. [17] By this is love perfected with
us, so that we may have confidence for the day of judgment, because as he is so also are we
in this world. [18] There is no fear in love, but perfect love casts out fear. For fear has to do
with punishment, and whoever fears has not been perfected in love. [19] We love because he
first loved us. [20] If anyone says, "I love God," and hates his brother, he is a liar; for he who
does not love his brother whom he has seen cannot love God whom he has not seen. [21] And
this commandment we have from him: whoever loves God must also love his brother.

We are to abound in love and grace to a fallen world.

And to that we are to give glory to God. We always need to remind ourselves of that action. We praise and honor God in everything we say, do, or think.

Paul loved these Macedonians. They were, in a way, gifts directly from God. Paul had wanted to travel to and minister in the regions of northern Asia Minor (modern-day Turkey). Still, God drove him to go instead to Macedonia and the Greek peninsula. And these Philippians became a gift to Paul, literally and figuratively.

And Paul rejoiced because of them.

So, before you start or continue with a project involving people, regardless of their standing with God, will you pray specifically for them? Taking a few minutes to pray makes all the difference in the universe. That's what Jesus did. That's what Paul did. That's what we ought to do.

Finding Joy: Philippians, Pray First

Verses: Acts 16:6-40, Philippians 1:1-11

Key Questions:

What's so special about Philippi?

Why do we need to pray for others?

Why Philippi:

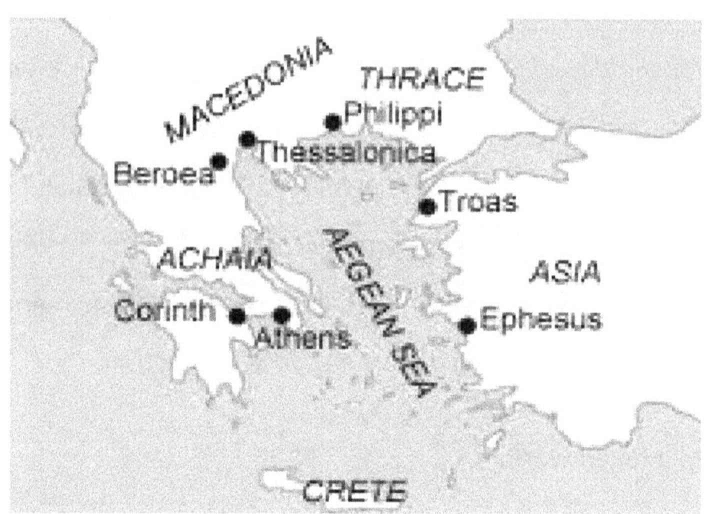

Purposely Praying for People:

E

I

R

Homework: Think about how you're praying for others. Continue praying for others by name.

Finding Joy: Homesick

What is it about "home" that we long for?

We love going on vacations or business trips, or visiting family and friends, but after some time, whether it's short or long, it's time to go home.

I remember as a child, we used to pack up Dad's big Oldsmobile sedan and head to Florida for about 2 weeks every February during winter break. Yes, winter break was only one week according to the school calendar. Still, my parents would take my brother and me out of school (after getting a folder full of make-up work) for that extra time and go away to get away from the business and the Connecticut winter.

Was there excitement about reaching our destination? Of course. But by the middle of the second week away, it was time to go home. As the miles went by and we got closer, there was more anticipation, almost as much as when we first left to go away. Now the anticipation was to get HOME. To sleep in our own beds, use our own bathrooms, and play in our own yards.

There's something about HOME.

Paul's letter to the Philippians speaks of a certain "homesickness". A certain longing for that place that you know you really belong with people who you not only love, but love you. Chapter one of the book of Philippians finishes up this way:

[12] I want you to know, brothers, that what has happened to me has really served to advance the gospel, [13] so that it has become known throughout the whole imperial guard and to all the rest that my imprisonment is for Christ. [14] And most of the brothers, having become confident in the Lord by my imprisonment, are much more bold to speak the word without fear.

[15] Some indeed preach Christ from envy and rivalry, but others from good will. [16] The latter
do it out of love, knowing that I am put here for the defense of the gospel. [17] The former
proclaim Christ out of selfish ambition, not sincerely but thinking to afflict me in my
imprisonment. [18] What then? Only that in every way, whether in pretense or in truth, Christ
is proclaimed, and in that I rejoice.

To Live Is Christ

Yes, and I will rejoice, [19] for I know that through your prayers and the help of the Spirit of
Jesus Christ this will turn out for my deliverance, [20] as it is my eager expectation and hope
that I will not be at all ashamed, but that with full courage now as always Christ will be
honored in my body, whether by life or by death. [21] For to me to live is Christ, and to die is
gain. [22] If I am to live in the flesh, that means fruitful labor for me. Yet which I shall choose I
cannot tell. [23] I am hard pressed between the two. My desire is to depart and be with Christ,
for that is far better. [24] But to remain in the flesh is more necessary on your account.
[25] Convinced of this, I know that I will remain and continue with you all, for your progress
and joy in the faith, [26] so that in me you may have ample cause to glory in Christ Jesus,
because of my coming to you again.

[27] Only let your manner of life be worthy of the gospel of Christ, so that whether I come and
see you or am absent, I may hear of you that you are standing firm in one spirit, with one
mind striving side by side for the faith of the gospel, [28] and not frightened in anything by
your opponents. This is a clear sign to them of their destruction, but of your salvation, and
that from God. [29] For it has been granted to you that for the sake of Christ you should not
only believe in him but also suffer for his sake, [30] engaged in the same conflict that you saw I
had and now hear that I still have. Philippians 1:12-30.

When we come to Christ, when we are adopted into God's eternal family as heirs to the Kingdom, we develop a longing for Home. And like Paul, we are torn between the two worlds. Our "natural" or "sinful" self desires to be here among the so-called living. It is familiar, it is comfortable. On the other hand, our "supernatural" or "saved" self knows that there's something much better, wildly better than here.

Several weeks after I first wrote this piece, I was heading out to Seattle. My daughter's husband at the time was deployed with the rest of his company, heading to Afghanistan. (Please continue to keep these men and women in your prayers, even today.) My job was to bring my daughter, grandson, and their dog home to Connecticut during his deployment. As the miles passed, heading east across the United States, the anticipation grew. We spent a day or two in Wisconsin visiting and resting a bit with my daughter's in-laws. Then there was the last major leg of the drive to HOME.

Each mile from Wisconsin to Connecticut sped by. Going through Pennsylvania, then New Jersey, and especially New York was familiar territory to my driving senses. Then there's the Connecticut Turnpike. We arrived through the night with just the streetlights to show us the way home. Then we got onto Route 8 north for the last 15 minutes. My grandson Caleb woke up after many miles and hours. Bethany and I were able to taste home.

Home is where our hearts lie and rest. We are relieved when we arrive home. We feel welcome. There is a certain relief when you pull in the driveway and walk through the kitchen door. Depending on the hour, someone will welcome us home.

And yet, we are called to toil on this earth. God has created every one of us with a purpose in mind. In the passage above, we can see that Paul is conflicted. Let's face it, over his years of ministry to a vastly pagan and unbelieving world, he is tired. He wants to go home. To a certain degree, he's had enough. Enough of the cursing. Enough of the beatings. Enough of the times at sea or countless miles literally traipsing through the Mediterranean world. Paul suffered cold, wind, heat, and rough seas. He suffered the mocking and unmitigated disrespect from people he was only trying to love.

That sounds a lot like what Jesus suffered through, doesn't it? Jesus had His eyes and His heart set like flint toward completing the race He had to run (we'll speak of this in greater depth when we get to Philippians chapter 3). His goal was the Cross, but ultimately, Jesus' goal was Home; to be back at the Father's side where He belonged. The Cross was completely necessary, and thankfully, He kept that at the forefront, but it was to be back in full union with the Father and the Holy Spirit. There was a job to do, a job to complete, but then at its completion, He could and would be Home.

I suspect that even Jesus (in His human nature) was "conflicted"; He experienced the same temptations and emotions that we experience (see Hebrews 2:17-18, 4:15). I'm sure He truly loved being with and interacting with His creation. He not only saw us in our frailties, but He directly experienced those frailties. Paul, like Jesus, labored on this earth and was to be very fruitful. Whatever we do when it is in the Father's Will and Plan is always fruitful. As direct partakers in God's Plan, there is much joy as we not only pray through it but also become an integral part of it. We give glory and praise to the Father in the unfolding of the Plan, and He graciously allows us to partake in the joy. My words fail me as I try to express these Truths.

Paul was conflicted. Read how the great apostle struggles physically, emotionally and spiritually. [21] *For to me to live is Christ, and to die is gain.* [22] *If I am to live in the flesh, that means fruitful labor for me. Yet which I shall choose I cannot tell.* [23] *I am hard pressed between the two. My desire is to depart and be with Christ, for that is far better.* [24] *But to remain in the flesh is more necessary on your account.* [25] *Convinced of this, I know that I will remain and continue with you all, for your progress and joy in the faith,* [26] *so that in me you may have ample cause to glory in Christ Jesus, because of my coming to you again.* Philippians 1:21-26

We remember that Paul wrote this letter while in captivity in Rome, in house arrest rather than prison, but in captivity nonetheless. We already spoke of the physical toll of his years on the missionary road. The emotional and spiritual anguish are just as grueling. He writes about the conflict going on in his mind.

As much as he would like to be back in Philippi with the church and his brothers and sisters in Christ, Paul knows that there is much work left to do, even in the Imperial household where he was held captive. It is God's Work and God's Word that must continue. And yet you can tell that he's tired and wants to go home. Living is Christ - the speaking and the healing and the general doing. Dying would be a true gain because he would leave this physical life behind and be in direct communion with his Lord.

Many years earlier, God had instructed Paul. He gave him a brief "walk-through" of heaven (2 Corinthians 12:2). He personally experienced all of the wonders of being in the direct presence of the Almighty. His entire being longed to go back, but not yet. As Paul notes, [24] *But to remain in the flesh is more necessary on your account."* He understood his place in the Gospel profession to the world, and, as much as he would have preferred to be at Jesus' direct side, Paul was fully content to continue his work. I think he would know when it was time to go home. God would let him know, and now was not the time.

And so, what would Paul do? He was "stranded" here, but with a Divine Mission. Paul also knew that every one of us who would choose to follow Jesus, like him, would need to take up the Savior's yoke. Jesus' yoke is easy. Jesus helps us with the yoke. Paul's (the Lord's, really) instructions are quite simple:

[27] *Only let your manner of life be worthy of the gospel of Christ, so that whether I come and see you or am absent, I may hear of you that you are standing firm in one spirit, with one mind striving side by side for the faith of the gospel,* [28] *and not frightened in anything by your opponents. This is a clear sign to them of their destruction, but of your salvation, and that from God.* [29] *For it has been granted to you that for the sake of Christ you should not only believe in him but also suffer for his sake,* [30] *engaged in the same conflict that you saw I had and now hear that I still have.* Philippians 1:27-30

We've all heard the cliché, "so heavenly minded that we're no earthly good". That's NOT what God has called us to be. Although Paul had his mind on heaven, he knew beyond the shadow of doubt that he was to be "earthly good" for God's purposes and glory. In fact, maybe we're to be so heavenly-minded that we are transformed to the degree that the unsaved are begging to have what we have.

Being stranded isn't necessarily a bad thing. The problem is that most of us are so used to being "busy", we forget that being down or put out of place can be a great time of renewal. So, what do we do?

First, we are to conduct ourselves in a Godly fashion. The yet unsaved world should see a reflection of Jesus when they look at us. Our actions and words speak to the greatness of God and the Gospel of Christ.

Then, we are to stand firm. Over and over again in the Bible, God tells us to "stand firm." And you know what? With a solid Rock foundation of the Word of God, it is much easier to stand firm, isn't it? There may be tremors from time to time, but we can stand firm.

Then we are to strive together for the Gospel. We need to link arms with other brothers and sisters in Christ, wherever they are in whatever circumstance they or we are in. When we stand firm and strive together, it is less difficult to be afraid of what unbelievers may say or think of us. Our God is so much greater! And after all, which is more to be afraid of: man or God?

Finally, as we conduct ourselves well, stand firm, and strive together, God saves us. We can't save us, but God CAN. That's the best news in the universe! That is the Gospel: God comes to earth to rescue us from our sinful selves and provides eternal life to those who believe and accept His free gift of salvation through the shedding of His sacrificial blood on the Cross.

When all is said and done, we'll get our one-way ticket home to the mansion that God is preparing and has prepared for each of us. Yes, a one-way ticket.

The night that I originally wrote this chapter, I had my one-way ticket to fly to Seattle, Washington, at the end of October 2012. Then with my daughter, grandson, and wonder dog Hunter, we began our journey home. The welcome, 3,000-plus miles later, will be good. It will be good to be home, surrounded by family.

In six months or so, the troops would be experiencing their own homecoming after living and fighting in a far-off, foreign land and would be reunited with their spouses, children, friends, and comrades. We all have jobs to do. We all have others who have gone on before us and are waiting for us to come home.

Heaven will be the same, but different, and we'll know that it's HOME. We'll know that this is where we belong. We've known it all along.

Finding Joy: Philippians, Homesick

Verses: Philippians 1:12 – 30

Key Questions:

What is the importance of "Christ being preached"?

How are we to be "heavenly minded" and "earthly good"?

Paul in chains & in conflict:

So, since we're stranded here:

C

S

S

S

Homework: How are you striving to live as well as present the Gospel to those in your sphere of influence?

Finding Joy: Attitude Adjustment

So..., how's your attitude?

And if you're offended by that question, then you have every right in the world to ask me about mine. And I wish you would!

So much of what each of us says, does, and thinks is directly tied to our own personal attitude. Our attitudes can be affected by our worldview or our particular circumstances. We may have certain prejudices or biases towards other people that prevent a solid, loving relationship, even if that relationship is "temporary," such as at a work or sales presentation, standing in line at the grocery store, or sitting in traffic with other commuters.

Our attitude determines almost every facet of our lives.

Our attitude also determines our ultimate "success" in living. Whether we "succeed" or "fail" depends on how positive or negative we are. Are we the little engine that "couldn't" or am I the little engine that COULD? "I think I can, I think I can ..." provides more of the positive "power" that projects me along to success and joy as opposed to "this (whatever this is) is impossible! I could never do it!" Remember what we've already said in other lessons - God asks us (almost demands) to do the impossible. And it's our attitude that will make all the difference.

Success is the goal or reward for a job well done, especially in the face of difficulty, with a good, persevering attitude. Love is an integral part of success. When you love doing something, the task - although perhaps difficult or impossible - is attainable. I often ask my students this rhetorical question: How do you eat an elephant. The answer is, you eat the elephant one bite at a time. That is how Jesus did everything in His life. He did everything with love and for pleasing God, one task, miracle, personal appearance, or encounter at a time.

Failure is the consequence of a job poorly performed without care or love. You don't care about yourself or the other person or people that may be affected. Everything is hollow about it. Hopefully, we learn from that failure and not repeat it in the future.

In the second chapter of Paul's epistle to the Philippian church, the apostle writes the following:

So if there is any encouragement in Christ, any comfort from love, any participation in the
Spirit, any affection and sympathy, [2] complete my joy by being of the same mind, having the
same love, being in full accord and of one mind. [3] Do nothing from selfish ambition or
conceit, but in humility count others more significant than yourselves. [4] Let each of you look
not only to his own interests, but also to the interests of others.

[5] *Have this mind among yourselves, which is yours in Christ Jesus,*
[6] *who, though he was in the form of God,*
did not count equality with God a thing to be grasped,
[7] *but emptied himself, by taking the form of a servant,*
being born in the likeness of men.
[8] *And being found in human form,*
he humbled himself by becoming obedient to the point of death,
even death on a cross.
[9] *Therefore God has highly exalted him*
and bestowed on him the name that is above every name,
[10] *so that at the name of Jesus every knee should bow,*
in heaven and on earth and under the earth,
[11] *and every tongue confess that Jesus Christ is Lord,*
to the glory of God the Father. Philippians 2:1-11.

Please note: verses 5-11 appear as one paragraph along with the preceding verses in the ESV. I've taken the liberty to break those sentences up for easier reading and hopefully deeper comprehension.

Let's briefly unpack these verses, then we'll make some applications.

Right away, Paul speaks of Love. Love and the Godly grace that powers love make or allow everything to work according to God's plan. Love and grace are the natural engines of encouragement, tenderness, and compassion: humility and other-centeredness help to provide everyone involved with joy.

Think of the last time you did something nice or helpful for someone - especially if they didn't know they were to have it done. If you did it - whatever it is - to be an encouragement for the other person or with tenderness and compassion, and then you did this task the way that the other person would like to have it done rather than your way, there's joy all the way around.

Just look at how love is integral to all of this. We should allow Scripture to help us better understand and interpret Scripture.

We learn about the dimensions of love from another one of the Apostle Paul's letters. Here's a passage used in many weddings, and it's very familiar. 1 Corinthians 13:1-13 reads like this:

If I speak in the tongues of men and of angels, but have not love, I am a noisy gong or a clanging cymbal. [2] *And if I have prophetic powers, and understand all mysteries and all knowledge, and if I have all faith, so as to remove mountains, but have not love, I am nothing.* [3] *If I give away all I have, and if I deliver up my body to be burned, but have not love, I gain nothing.*

[4] *Love is patient and kind; love does not envy or boast; it is not arrogant* [5] *or rude. It does not insist on its own way; it is not irritable or resentful;* [6] *it does not rejoice at wrongdoing, but rejoices with the truth.* [7] *Love bears all things, believes all things, hopes all things, endures all things.*

[8] Love never ends. As for prophecies, they will pass away; as for tongues, they will cease; as for knowledge, it will pass away. [9] For we know in part and we prophesy in part, [10] but when the perfect comes, the partial will pass away. [11] When I was a child, I spoke like a child, I thought like a child, I reasoned like a child. When I became a man, I gave up childish ways. [12] For now we see in a mirror dimly, but then face to face. Now I know in part; then I shall know fully, even as I have been fully known.

[13] So now faith, hope, and love abide, these three; but the greatest of these is love.

Whatever God does, He does out of complete and perfect love.

Now what of all this love stuff? We have two ideas to consider. After all, Paul is essentially telling the Philippian church - and all of us today - look at yourselves and your relationships to one another. Be like Jesus! Act like Jesus! We are to have the same "attitude" as Jesus.

The first idea is that we are to be Imitators of Jesus. Jesus was and is our model for life and living. To live a successful and abundant life, we must imitate Him. Although Jesus is God (we'll address the aspect of Jesus Deity in another lesson, using this same passage), that's not the way He "acted" when He walked among us two thousand years ago.

Instead of "lording" His Lordship over us, which He had every right to do being God, Jesus condescended. Jesus put off or put aside His Deity (but not His Divinity) and dwelt with mortal men and women. Jesus experienced everything that you and I experience. He knows how hard life can be. Yet out of love, He yearns that we imitate His life as best as possible; He knows that we're not perfect.

In other words, we are to become servants just like Jesus was. Even Jesus said that He came to serve rather than be served (Matthew 20:28 and Mark 10:45).

And not only are we to be as servants, but Jesus also guaranteed us a life of hardship. He never said it was going to be easy! Paul describes his life of hardship, all the while persevering out of a desire to be a good imitator of Jesus. Because Paul loved God first and the people to whom he was called to minister, the apostle could indeed imitate and endure.

In 2 Corinthians 6, we read:

[3] We put no obstacle in anyone's way, so that no fault may be found with our ministry, [4] but as servants of God we commend ourselves in every way: by great endurance, in afflictions, hardships, calamities, [5] beatings, imprisonments, riots, labors, sleepless nights, hunger; [6] by purity, knowledge, patience, kindness, the Holy Spirit, genuine love; [7] by truthful speech, and the power of God; with the weapons of righteousness for the right hand and for the left; [8] through honor and dishonor, through slander and praise. We are treated as impostors, and yet are true; [9] as unknown, and yet well known; as dying, and behold, we live; as punished, and yet not killed; 2 Corinthians 6:3-9

And notice those last couple of verses; look at the joy and the success. Through all of the hardship and pain, it seemed as if Paul had nothing. Yet because this little Jewish guy, chosen by God to do a great (and somewhat impossible) task, imitated Jesus, he would possess eternal life; he would (and we will too) possess everything because of the generosity of the Father. That's what imitating Jesus brings!

Plus, we do these things because of what Paul writes in verse two, *"Behold, now is the favorable time; behold, now is the day of salvation."* None of us knows what tomorrow, or even the next hour, may bring. As believers, God calls us to join Him in making heaven crowded. My poor attitude towards some will prevent that from happening, whereas a Christ-like attitude will be fruitful.

Because Jesus condescended and became obedient even to death (Philippians 2:8), God the Father then exalted Jesus to the Highest Place (Philippians 2:9). And we remember that it is God who does the exalting; we don't. This is God's Plan and Story, not ours. We are to Imitate Jesus out of Love. We are to die to ourselves so that God can resurrect us to an abundant life of Godly living (Galatians 2:20). Love for God as well as love for our fellow man.

The second path, driven by Love, is to be one who is Reconciled.

As we have been reconciled to God by our believing and accepting the finished work of Jesus on the Cross, so too are we to be reconciled one to another. Our passage today in Philippians may not explicitly state or express this reconciliation, but it's there implicitly. After all, why did Jesus come as He did? Why is it so necessary that we imitate Christ?

We imitate Jesus in order for you and me to be reconciled to God. Jesus had to die a cruel death. Sin had (has) to be punished. There is nothing any one of us can do to merit any standing at all with God. Our best offerings to Him are as filthy rags (Isaiah 64:6). Our motives are impure. Our acts are even less! And still God wants us to be reconciled to Him. Only Love can ask for that to be done. Only Jesus' atoning death can bring that about.

But what about being reconciled to one another? Reconciliation is a two-way street (like Forgiveness). Our love for one another ought to drive us to be reconciled. We are reconciled to one another in God's eyes. Again, let's look at 2 Corinthians. In chapter five, we read:

16 From now on, therefore, we regard no one according to the flesh. Even though we once regarded Christ according to the flesh, we regard him thus no longer. 17 Therefore, if anyone is in Christ, he is a new creation. The old has passed away; behold, the new has come. 18 All this is from God, who through Christ reconciled us to himself and gave us the ministry of reconciliation; 19 that is, in Christ God was reconciling the world to himself, not counting their trespasses against them, and entrusting to us the message of reconciliation. 20 Therefore, we are ambassadors for Christ, God making his appeal through us. We implore you on behalf of Christ, be reconciled to God. 2 Corinthians 5:16-20.

As ambassadors, we are to be direct representatives for God on this earth. We have a divinely appointed job to present God and His Gospel of reconciliation to a lost and dying world. Yes, God speaks through Nature and His Word, but He has called us to be His hands and feet, mouths and ears to people who will not look at the world around them, or pick up a copy of the Bible, or listen to a Christian music station, or darken the door of a church.

Our job is first to make sure that we are reconciled to God. Once that is secure, we are to be reconciled to one another, and that doesn't mean unbelievers. If we can't be properly reconciled to our brothers and sisters in Christ, then how are we to be reconciled to those who have nothing spiritually in common with us? Now that's really impossible. Our reconciliation must start in our own homes and workplaces and then spread out from there.

We began this series in the book of Philippians, stating that it is the book of "Joy". How true! Truth be told, we're learning that joy is the outcome of so many other things.

Having a change of attitude leads to many things; many good and Godly things. By changing our natural, selfish, self-centered attitude to one of love and grace, we more fully experience God. To more fully experience God in love, we need to, we must be imitators of Christ (Ephesians 5:1) in all that we do and persevere to do. It won't necessarily be easy, and yet His yoke is easy.

Our change to a loving attitude allows us to be reconciled to God. As we are reconciled to God, and as we imitate Jesus, we are reconciled to each other.

Reconciled in our homes between husbands and wives, parents and children.

Reconciled in our churches by seeking forgiveness and being forgiven, of and by fellow believers.

Reconciled in our places of work and school with those who may not share our values.

Reconciled to those who are marginalized in the society around us.

And all of this is done because of love.

Let's end with this reminder from Jesus Himself, the One Whom we are to imitate, the only One Who can reconcile us to God. I'm sure you know the verse. [16] *"For God so loved the world, that he gave his only Son, that whoever believes in him should not perish but have eternal life.* [17] *For God did not send his Son into the world to condemn the world, but in order that the world might be saved through him."* John 3:16-17.

And for that we have, and experience, much joy. Love brings about Joy.

Finding Joy: Philippians, Attitude Adjustment

Verses: Philippians 2:1 – 11, 1 Cor 13:1 – 13, 2 Cor 6:3 – 9, 2 Cor 5:16 – 20

Key Questions:

What does it mean "*Your attitude should be the same as that of Christ Jesus*"?

How are we to act having that attitude?

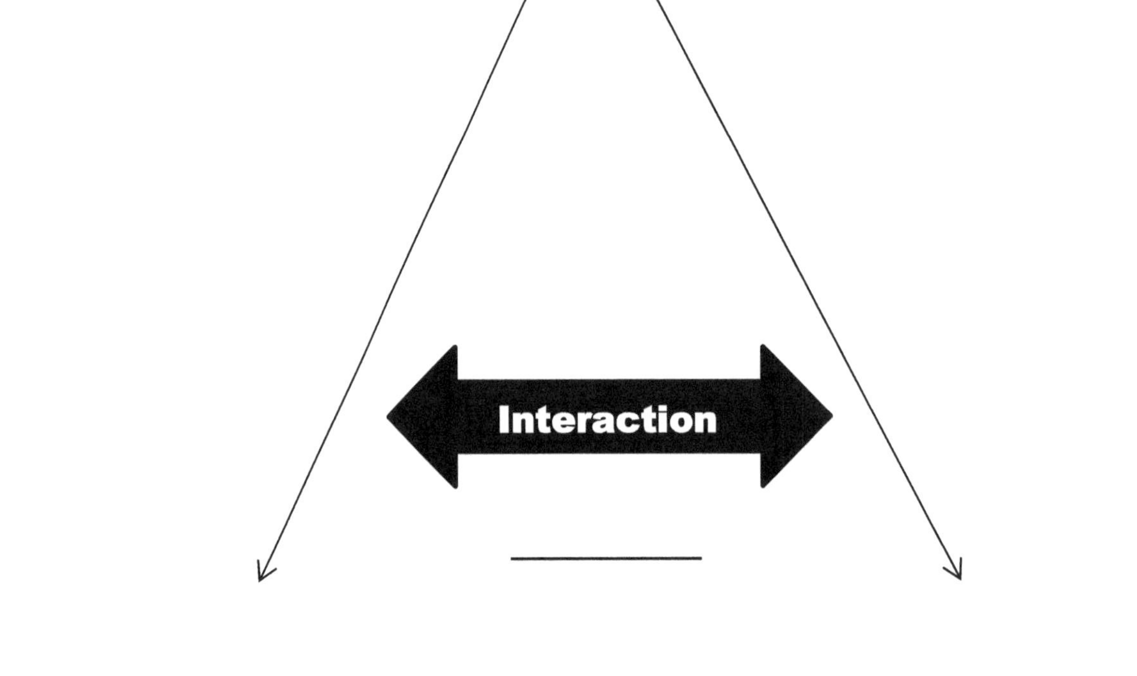

Homework: The Gospel is a mirror for our daily living. With every action & interaction, are we leading a successful & fruitful life because of a good attitude?

Finding Joy: Jesus Christ, His Deity and Humanity

Jesus Christ!

How you use those two words in general conversation speaks volumes about what you believe about those two words.

So, when you say "Jesus Christ," are you speaking in praise and worship of the King of the Universe, or are you speaking poorly, even obscenely, about something else? What's your attitude about that Name? Do you not care, or does it mean everything to you?

In fact, what comes to mind when you think of Jesus and God are the most important thoughts of your entire life. What you think - and therefore believe - about Who God is and what He has done, what He presently does, and what He will do, sets the tone for every aspect of your life both now and into eternity.

Jesus was named in the days when names really meant something to other people. Long ago, our given names were purposeful. People didn't have names just because they "sounded good." Names meant something special about the person, or the circumstances into which they were born, or a certain event involving them, or in memory of another person.

The name Jesus Christ is not simply two words. Those two words are the Name and Title of the Son of God, the second person, the Son, of the Triune Godhead. These names are not His first and last names. His Name is Jesus. His Title is Christ. The two words are anglicized Greek words: Jesus is the Greek form of the Hebrew name Yeshua or Joshua, meaning "God saves"; Christ is from Christos, the Greek translation of the Hebrew word "messhiach" or "messiah," meaning "anointed one".

Amazing! His Name tells us Who He is and what His mission was. You could say that Jesus Christ really means, "God the Anointed One saves." How true. Remember that God named Himself when the angel Gabriel (meaning God is my might or strong man of God; either title very appropriate for the archangel) announced to Mary that she would carry God's Son and that he would be named "Yeshua" or Jesus (Matthew 1:21). Centuries earlier, the prophet Isaiah prophesied that a virgin from Bethlehem of the House and lineage of David would bear a child and His name would be Immanuel or "God with us" (Isaiah 7:14). How apropos. Jesus, being very God of very God, came down from Heaven and lived with His creation, in the same physical form as His creation. What an astounding thought!

Today, many (most) non-Christians in our post-modern, post-Christian, secular-leaning Western society, believe that Jesus was, at best, a good teacher. He was a "godly" man. He was a prophet (something that Muslims believe). Jesus is a good example of how to live and treat other people. All of these are very true, but the reason why these people are not truly Christians is that they do not believe in Jesus' deity. They prefer subjective truth and reject objective absolutes. They choose not to believe in absolute good or evil, right or wrong, eternal bliss or eternal punishment. The virgin birth is explained away, and Jesus's bodily resurrection is either ignored or denied. Some would even deny His very historical existence, regardless of the literal mountains of evidence.

The fact of the matter is that there is more evidence for everything about Jesus' birth, life, ministry, death, and resurrection than for anyone else who has ever lived on planet earth. The evidence for Jesus' existence is chronicled in document after document dating back almost 2000 years, as well as in "experiential" accounts. As a result, the birth, life, ministry, death, and resurrection of Jesus has affected more people over the centuries than any one person in all of human history. He has changed lives and continues to do so every day, in every part of the world.

Jesus IS God.

In the New Testament, we find two passages that brilliantly describe this Jesus. The Apostle Paul, under the inspiration of the Holy Spirit, writes perfectly explaining that Jesus is fully God and fully man. Paul was completely convinced of that fact. The problem is that it is a hard fact to understand. It is beyond human comprehension.

Paul understood that Jesus, as God Incarnate, completely condescended to humanity so that He might restore the relationship that was shattered at the Fall in the Garden of Eden. Jesus was the only One who could atone for my sins and your sins; no one else or nothing else would suffice. Let's look at these two passages.

The first passage, we've already looked at:

Christ Jesus,
6 *who, though he was in the form of God,*
did not count equality with God a thing to be grasped,
7 *but emptied himself, by taking the form of a servant,*
being born in the likeness of men.
8 *And being found in human form,*
he humbled himself by becoming obedient to the point of death,
even death on a cross.
9 *Therefore God has highly exalted him*
and bestowed on him the name that is above every name,
10 *so that at the name of Jesus every knee should bow,*
in heaven and on earth and under the earth,
11 *and every tongue confess that Jesus Christ is Lord,*
to the glory of God the Father. Philippians 2:6-11

The next passage we find in the opening verses of the epistle to the Hebrews:

Long ago, at many times and in many ways, God spoke to our fathers by the prophets, 2 *but*
in these last days he has spoken to us by his Son, whom he appointed the heir of all things,
through whom also he created the world. 3 *He is the radiance of the glory of God and the*
exact imprint of his nature, and he upholds the universe by the word of his power. After
making purification for sins, he sat down at the right hand of the Majesty on high, 4 *having*
become as much superior to angels as the name he has inherited is more excellent than
theirs. Hebrews 1:1-4 (exact author unknown)

Hebrews chapter one goes on to tell more about Jesus and how He is not an angel or any other created being. Jesus is unequivocally GOD.

Jesus is the "hypostasis" in which His human and divine natures are completely united and inseparable. Hypostatis or the "hypostatic (personal) union" is the understanding that Jesus's one personality is the union of His two natures (human and divine). Each member of the Trinity, Father, Son, and Holy Spirit, are individuals, and are God. It is a personal union, as God is a personal God. Between the 4th and 5th centuries AD (or CE - Christian or common era), there was great discussion between two primary schools of Christian thought, unfortunately resulting in three heresies. The Antiochene school, which taught that Jesus could be either man or God at one time, not both; the Alexandrian school proposed that Jesus was not completely human, and that His divine nature was more important. The Arian heresy taught that He was a figurative son, like the other "sons of God" in the Bible (also found in certain of today's cults), a created being, not the Son of God.

The doctrine of the Deity of Jesus Christ is the bedrock foundation to the Christian faith. Without Jesus being fully God and fully man, everything that He did would have been fruitless and even futile. Reducing Jesus to a "miracle worker" (even Satan can perform miracles), a "good teacher" (there have been many "good" teachers throughout history), or a "prophet" (there have been hundreds of prophets over the ages), nullifies the salvific work of His crucifixion, and bodily resurrection. The only way that humanity, and all of creation itself, could be redeemed and reconciled to God would be if Jesus was and is 100% Deity and human at the same time (fully God and fully man).

At the Council of Nicaea in 325 AD, a creed (defined as a formal written statement of belief or a confession of faith) was written to explain God, Jesus, His atoning work, the Holy Spirit, and the doctrine of the Trinity. This creed is known today as the Nicene Creed. One of the theologians present at the Council, Athanasius, didn't think that the creed went far enough in stating Jesus' Deity and Divinity. Athanasius was a man of many words. He was the secretary to Bishop Alexander of Alexandria, and didn't think the "official" creed went far enough. I would recommend reading the two creeds side by side for the full flavor. You'll find these at the conclusion of this chapter. Please read and reread them prayerfully.

Later at the Council of Chalcedon in 451 AD, - in the Confession of Chalcedon – a further clarification was made with just two tiny words. The clarification was that Jesus was IN two natures rather than OF two natures. IN signifying that Jesus has the two natures of God and man, always and at the same time. How could that be? Well, when you are God and are eternal, omniscient, omnipresent, omnipotent, and exist outside of time and space, you can do just about anything. OF signifies something being "bestowed" on Him; these attributes are not and were not always a part of Him. Two little words which convey a significant difference.

When it comes to God, we must always be exact in how we understand and relate to Him. He (not she or some other neutral and erroneous idea) is, has been, and always will be God. Words count, and those little words sometimes even more so.

This confession is what is known as the "homo-ousian". Jesus is of the same (homo) nature or essence as God. It is impossible to fully explain, understand, comprehend, and think about Who God is. It will take an eternity to know Him, and we've already missed eternity past in the process.

Let's look at the mathematics of being Jesus Christ. Being God, Jesus did not add anything to Himself. He is already complete. He always has been complete. Knowing (ready for your head to explode?) that we men and women are created in God's Image, this isn't "difficult" (while also being glorious) to understand...

Jesus, being conceived of the Holy Spirit, was the adopted son of Joseph (He would have been known as Joshua bar Joseph), He did not subtract anything from who He already was (from eternity past), is, and always will be. Instead, Jesus, the Son of God, the second Person of the Trinity, chose - He CHOSE - to temporarily put aside parts of His divine nature and condescend to humanity for the purpose of interacting with us and ultimately being the ONLY sacrifice that God would accept for the atoning of our sins (Romans 6:10, Colossians 1:19-22, Hebrews 7:27, 1 John 2:2). God demanded a perfect sacrifice for the removal of our sins. Man could never provide one. It was impossible. Bulls, goats, and anything else were a completely feeble sacrifice. Those creatures are animals - they are not created in the image of God. Animals are not God's image bearers. Only Man (men and women) is. I hate to belabor the point, but we MUST, and understand the significance of the sacrificial death of Jesus. Jesus is fully God and fully man. Jesus was the only and completely sinless man to ever walk the earth. Being sinless, only Jesus could be the sacrifice that God demanded for the restoration of our fellowship with Him.

Jesus was born human, setting aside His deity. He lived as a man, played as a child, worked as a carpenter's son in adulthood. He died as a man, fully bleeding out on the cross after suffering the scourging of the Roman guards, with the approval of the Jewish leadership. He rose from the dead with His glorified body, completely recognizable to all of His friends.

But back to the Name before we close this chapter. It is a glorious name. A name above every other name in heaven or on earth. A name, when proclaimed [10] *so that at the name of Jesus every knee should bow, in heaven and on earth and under the earth,* [11] *and every tongue confess that Jesus Christ is Lord, to the glory of God the Father.* (Philippians 2:10 - 11).

And so we are left with this choice: proclaim the Name of Jesus with glory, praise, and honor as your personal Lord and Savior, dwelling with Him in Heaven for all eternity, or acknowledge Him as someone other than Savior and He will be your Divine Judge forever in Hell for all eternity.

As a side note, Jesus says on several occasions that in Hell, there will be "weeping and gnashing of teeth." What does that mean? Who will be weeping? Those souls who will be weeping for all eternity, are those people who heard the Gospel, but walked away and said, "No, I don't need Jesus. He's a good teacher, but I don't need Jesus." Or, "I'll make a decision for Jesus tomorrow." And tomorrow never comes. Who will be gnashing their teeth? They are those who are always shaking their fists at God for a variety of reasons such as, "God's not fair!" or "Everybody ought to go to Heaven!" or "Sky-daddy is just a made-up belief." Both sets of people heard the presentation of the Gospel and chose to reject it. Imagine being in a place for all eternity where all that you hear is weeping and gnashing of teeth? Come to Jesus! Receive His gift of forgiveness, salvation, and eternal life with the loving God who created you.

We've only begun to scratch the surface of understanding Jesus. Make the time to read and study the entire Bible. You will find that Jesus is central in the pages of Biblical Scripture. You'll find Him in the opening verses of Genesis, through every book in the Old and New Testaments, ending in His glorious return in the Book of the Revelation of Jesus Christ.

In the end, each of us has to make a decision about Jesus. Either He is Who He says He is or He's not. That fact has been so for almost 2,000 years. The religious leaders of that time struggled with that question. Read John 11:45-53. Their "wrong" choice fulfilled prophecy. Our wrong choice will determine our eternity.

Let's conclude this chapter in a word of prayer.

Lord God, we are humbled even greater when we begin to understand Who You are and what You have done for us. It is amazing! Our feeble minds can only begin to learn and grasp just an inkling of Your Person. It is beyond our comprehension. Thankfully, You love us anyway. You love us because we have been created by You. You have saved us because we have individually believed that You died and rose again to take away our individual sins. That's something that we could have never done. Lord, we pray that You continue to give us an eternal thirst to know and love You. Continue to open my mind to Your Glory and Majesty. We wait with great anticipation for our reunion with You. It's in the magnificent Name of Jesus that we pray. Amen.

The Nicene Creed

We believe in one God the Father, the Almighty,
maker of heaven and earth, of all that is, seen and unseen.

We believe in one Lord, Jesus Christ, the only Son of God,
eternally begotten of the Father,
God from God, Light from Light, true God from true God,
begotten, not made, of one Being with the Father;
through him all things were made.
For us and for our salvation he came down from heaven,
was incarnate of the Holy Spirit and the Virgin Mary
and became truly human.
For our sake he was crucified under Pontius Pilate;
he suffered death and was buried.
On the third day he rose again in accordance
with the Scriptures;
he ascended into heaven and is seated at the right hand
of the Father.
He will come again in glory to judge the living and the dead,
and his kingdom will have no end.

We believe in the Holy Spirit, the Lord, and the giver of life,
who proceeds from the Father and the Son,
who with the Father and the Son is worshiped and glorified,
who has spoken through the prophets.
We believe in the one holy catholic (universal Christian) and apostolic church.
We acknowledge one baptism for the forgiveness of sins.
We look for the resurrection of the dead,
and the life of the world to come. Amen.

Athanasian Creed (catholic = universal Christian)

Whoever wants to be saved should above all cling to the catholic faith.

Whoever does not guard it whole and inviolable will doubtless perish eternally.

Now this is the catholic faith: We worship one God in trinity and the Trinity in unity, neither confusing the persons nor dividing the divine being.

For the Father is one person, the Son is another, and the Spirit is still another.

But the deity of the Father, Son, and Holy Spirit is one, equal in glory, coeternal in majesty.

What the Father is, the Son is, and so is the Holy Spirit.

Uncreated is the Father; uncreated is the Son; uncreated is the Spirit.

The Father is infinite; the Son is infinite; the Holy Spirit is infinite.

Eternal is the Father; eternal is the Son; eternal is the Spirit: And yet there are not three eternal beings, but one who is eternal; as there are not three uncreated and unlimited beings, but one who is uncreated and unlimited.

Almighty is the Father; almighty is the Son; almighty is the Spirit: And yet there are not three almighty beings, but one who is almighty.

Thus the Father is God; the Son is God; the Holy Spirit is God: And yet there are not three gods, but one God.

Thus the Father is Lord; the Son is Lord; the Holy Spirit is Lord: And yet there are not three lords, but one Lord.

As Christian truth compels us to acknowledge each distinct person as God and Lord, so catholic religion forbids us to say that there are three gods or lords.

The Father was neither made nor created nor begotten; the Son was neither made nor created, but was alone begotten of the Father; the Spirit was neither made nor created, but is proceeding from the Father and the Son.

Thus there is one Father, not three fathers; one Son, not three sons; one Holy Spirit, not three spirits.

And in this Trinity, no one is before or after, greater or less than the other; but all three persons are in themselves, coeternal and coequal; and so we must worship the Trinity in unity and the one God in three persons.

Whoever wants to be saved should think thus about the Trinity.

It is necessary for eternal salvation that one also faithfully believe that our Lord Jesus Christ became flesh.

For this is the true faith that we believe and confess: That our Lord Jesus Christ, God's Son, is both God and man.

He is God, begotten before all worlds from the being of the Father, and he is man, born in the world from the being of his mother -- existing fully as God, and fully as man with a rational soul and a human body; equal to the Father in divinity, subordinate to the Father in humanity.

Although he is God and man, he is not divided, but is one Christ.

He is united because God has taken humanity into himself; he does not transform deity into humanity.

He is completely one in the unity of his person, without confusing his natures.

For as the rational soul and body are one person, so the one Christ is God and man.

He suffered death for our salvation. He descended into hell and rose again from the dead.

He ascended into heaven and is seated at the right hand of the Father.

He will come again to judge the living and the dead.

At his coming all people shall rise bodily to give an account of their own deeds.

Those who have done good will enter eternal life, those who have done evil will enter eternal fire.

This is the catholic faith.

One cannot be saved without believing this firmly and faithfully.

Finding Joy: Philippians, Jesus Christ, His Deity and Humanity

Verses: Philippians 2:6 – 11, Hebrews 1:1-4

Key Questions:

What does it mean that Jesus is fully God and fully man?

Why is it important that Jesus is fully God and fully man? What if He wasn't?

What do we do with Jesus? Is He your Lord and Savior or not?

Discussion:

Discuss the above 2 questions.

Read and discuss the 2 creeds found at the end of the chapter.

Terms to be familiar with:

Hypostasis or Hypostatic –

Homo-ousian –

Expiation vs. Propitiation

Expiation –

Propitiation –

Doctrine of the Kenosis – what did God the Son do to become Jesus the Christ?

Kenosis –

The Problem of the God-Man – the mathematics of the problem

Addition –

Subtraction –

Choice –

What are the struggles that we have today regarding Jesus?

Proofs of Jesus' Humanity – list the various Bible passages

1. Human body –
2. Human soul & spirit –
3. Human characteristics –
4. Possessed human names –

Why Jesus? - Proofs of Jesus' deity

1. In His Incarnation –

2. In His Ministry –

3. In His Death & Resurrection –

So, what do we do with Jesus? How do you respond to the Gospel?

John 11:45 – 53

Finding Joy: Shine

Are you an older brother or sister? Are you in some way a leader – be it of a family, company or some other type of organization?

If you are, you've probably heard the admonishment to not only be an example for others, but to be a "shining" example for others.

The word shining connotes the idea of being attractive or something to strive for: to be the "best" of whatever it is that you are exemplifying. That's not easy. It's not easy to always be the "best". What's worse is that over time, some people actually disdain you. You get called names like "goodie two-shoes" or "teacher's pet." You know who you are. You may not have minded it, but let's be frank: sometimes it wasn't fun; it was tiring. You felt like you were always under a microscope or that others were constantly holding a checklist up to your life.

When you had had enough, you wanted to break free of that mold and just be yourself. You wanted to be "fallible," especially if this shining example were as a sibling. Not only were you keeping up appearances for mom and dad, but you had to deal with the brother or sister who wasn't as shiny or squeaky clean as you. There was always this balance or tension that felt like a burden, a yoke to bear.

As much as you may have "measured up" to mom and dad or the boss or the teacher (and then yourself, because this whole mess turns onto itself), you were constantly working; constantly striving. And sometimes feeling that you were constantly failing instead. It may not have been all bad, but... Thankfully, as we mature, we can put these times of frustrating self-flagellation into better perspective.

So now what?

An attitude adjustment is one thing, but for what purpose? Yes, we are to be imitators of Christ and to be in the reconciliation business like Christ, but there's more. When we looked at the hows and whys of prayer, we discussed that having a vibrant prayer life, having a good and regular communion with God, would lead to a "shining" life that attracts and points people to Jesus and not ourselves. Will we be singled out as examples? Yes, but it is intended to redirect them to our source, or as the apostle Peter puts it, our reason for the hope that we have (1 Peter 3:15-16).

As we look at Philippians 2:12-18, we're going to take a closer look at a "why" - the "why" that we imitate and reconcile.

[12] Therefore, my beloved, as you have always obeyed, so now, not only as in my presence but much more in my absence, work out your own salvation with fear and trembling, [13] for it is God who works in you, both to will and to work for his good pleasure.

[14] Do all things without grumbling or disputing, [15] that you may be blameless and innocent,
children of God without blemish in the midst of a crooked and twisted generation, among
whom you shine as lights in the world, [16] holding fast to the word of life, so that in the day of
Christ I may be proud that I did not run in vain or labor in vain. [17] Even if I am to be poured
out as a drink offering upon the sacrificial offering of your faith, I am glad and rejoice with
you all. [18] Likewise you also should be glad and rejoice with me.

We'll go through the passage, but I really want to concentrate on that one word "shine" in verse 15.

Verse twelve is fun. Paul knows the old axiom that "when the cat's away, the mice will play." He reminds the Philippians that they are to work out their own salvation, more so in his absence. Why? Think about it...

If you have someone continually supervising and directing you, it's (whatever the task is) somewhat easy. But take away the supervision and direction, and it's suddenly all on you (me). And that's the whole point of the Gospel message and God's Plan of salvation: we are to be reconciled to God through the Cross of Jesus as *individuals*. We come as we are; alone, in private, baring all, being completely transparent. We don't come on our parents' background and coattails, or on grandma's prayers (although those may have been means to bring you to the Cross in the first place). We come to God alone. There is no "corporate" salvation.

That's one of the facts that differentiates Christianity from every other religious system. Until we come to Christ seeking forgiveness of sin and our personal sinful nature, we are enemies of God (Romans 5:10). We have no fellowship with Him at all. We cannot merit anything without first being reconciled, and even then, if we're only accepting Christ's forgiveness for the purpose of eternal fire insurance, what's the point? God sees right through that false piety (which in itself is sin).

The only thing that we're "working out in fear and trembling" is our becoming Christ-like. We (I or you) should be continually striving to look more like Jesus every hour of the day, every day of the week. But we remember that it is God working through us. God is the one Who brings light to our lives. We are utterly and thoroughly incapable of bringing light into the world, let alone our own darkness (see Matthew 6:23 and Luke 11:34). Only God Himself is light - true light.

All that said, Jesus gives us the command to *"let your light shine before others, that they may see your good works and give glory to your Father who is in heaven."* Matthew 5:16. It is necessary that we "shine" for God. He receives the glory He deserves, we receive the joy that He gives.

Ultimately, what does light do? What does this "shining" provide for our own lives and the Kingdom of God? I would propose three object lessons: personal transparency, the true darkness of the world around us being exposed, and the centrality of the Cross in the Gospel.

God is at work in our lives to bring about His Kingdom and His righteousness; to bring about reconciliation of the sinfulness of humanity to a pure and holy God and Creator. Our new lives as believers in Jesus Christ are for the glory of God's plan and purposes, not ours. Our plans are rubbish (we'll discuss that in a later chapter). God's purposes are always good; ours are evil and almost always self-serving. We are to "become blameless and pure" when contrasted to this "crooked and depraved" generation.

But that can only happen when we submit our individual lives and persons to the authority of Christ.

God's light and our shining first bring about personal transparency. Over the past several years, we've heard a lot about "transparency", but we rarely see it applied. Yes, it gets talked about. People want it. But do they really?

I don't know about you, but the thought of being "transparent" makes me nervous. Actually, it scares me to death that someone, maybe all of you, may or will find out things about me that are utterly embarrassing. My sins, my shortcomings, are beyond the dirty rags of good works that I can boast about.

As I work out my salvation with fear and trembling, I get really nervous about what will be vomited out. The Holy Spirit wants to take a toilet bowl brush and get under the rim of my life. Sorry to be so graphic, but that's what this is all about. God's light shining into my life will expose a lot of dirt, cobwebs, and more that I would rather keep hidden in a closet, away from prying eyes.

But when I am transparent, when God's light shines into my personal darkness, that junk is exposed so that the Holy Spirit can clean it out. I can confess and repent. Furthermore, as I confess, repent, and allow God's light to penetrate my life, it is purified by that light. Light (particularly invisible ultraviolet light) is a great and natural "purifier" that oxidizes and destroys impurities.

God's light shining in and through us exposes the true darkness of the world around us. Let's face it, how many times have you heard that all people are "generally good"? That, my friends, is an absolute lie directly out of the pit of hell! Being a father and grandfather, I can tell you that I (or my wife) did not have to teach any of our children or grandchildren how to sin. Sin was natural.

The Bible tells us that *"all have sinned and fall short of the glory of God"* (Romans 3:23) and that *"we all, like sheep, have gone astray, we have turned - everyone - to his* [or her*] own way"* (Isaiah 53:6). No one person in the world is *"good - except God alone."* (Mark 10:18).

What's worse - if that were possible - is that evil has become good and good evil. In fact, men and women *"love evil rather than good, and lying more than speaking what is right."* (Psalm 52:3). Today, as through all of history, men and women have always sought out their own pleasures and desires; our own wants. We are self-centered. Romans 1:18-25 is a glaring condemnation of our natural and sinful nature. And as we spiral down into our lusts, denying God and His righteousness in the process, we - and therefore society - become darker and darker.

Thankfully, just one point of light can do tremendous good in exposing this sin. That is our job as believers in Jesus Christ: to shine forth in a dark and dying world. Christians are supposed to be God's ambassadors in proclaiming His truth, not ours; His Word, not ours; His Light, not ours. We are to speak truth, life, and light wherever we have been placed - in geography and history. Regardless of home, school, workplace, vacation resort, or even in the church.

Our light - actually His light shining through us - casts away darkness and death. Unwillingly, darkness and death flee, making as much noise and commotion as possible. We are mocked and ridiculed, but it is all for the eternal light and glory of God and His Kingdom. Our individual and continuing response to Jesus determines how brightly we shine.

And this light distinguishes (or is supposed to) true Christians from everyone else. It's LOVE. Not the mushy love that people think they want, but God's love that includes justice, mercy, and personal sacrifice. Here's how the apostle John put it:

[7] Beloved, let us love one another, for love is from God, and whoever loves has been born of God and knows God. [8] Anyone who does not love does not know God, because God is love. [9] In this the love of God was made manifest among us, that God sent his only Son into the world, so that we might live through him. [10] In this is love, not that we have loved God but that he loved us and sent his Son to be the propitiation for our sins. [11] Beloved, if God so loved us, we also ought to love one another. [12] No one has ever seen God; if we love one another, God abides in us and his love is perfected in us. 1 John 4:7-12.

Finally, our shining reflection of God's light in our lives points the unbeliever to the Cross. That's the bottom line. The light shining through us is not to highlight who we are and what we've done, regardless of how "good" we may be or how "good" we may have done; this light is to be a beacon pointing directly to the Cross of Christ.

Paul writes in 2 Corinthians 4:4-6

[4] In their case the god of this world [Satan] *has blinded the minds of the unbelievers, to keep them from seeing the light of the gospel of the glory of Christ, who is the image of God. [5] For what we proclaim is not ourselves, but Jesus Christ as Lord, with ourselves as your servants for Jesus' sake. [6] For God, who said, "Let light shine out of darkness," has shone in our hearts to give the light of the knowledge of the glory of God in the face of Jesus Christ.*

As Greg Gilbert writes in his great little book *"What is the Gospel"* (powerful reading), the Church is nothing more than an "outpost" of the Kingdom of God. God showcases who He is through us. That's an amazing thought to comprehend!

People want to hear good news. They want a gospel. We are to bring them THE Gospel. And God's Gospel is not just that He is love and therefore cares for everyone (which is perfectly true). Nor is the Gospel our good works and helping our fellow man (the so-called social gospel). The centerpiece of the True Gospel of God is the Cross, that cruel instrument of torment and death on which was crucified the sins of all humankind for all ages. And Jesus is the One who came to earth, condescended from Divinity to live a fully human life (although perfect and without sin), and consented to die a substitutionary death for you and me. Jesus bore your sins and my sins and removed them from the Father's sight when we placed our trust in that death by faith alone. Not our works or our "righteousness" but His atoning death and subsequent bodily resurrection, which is a guarantee of our eternal life.

Only the Cross brings light - nothing else. Is there anything bigger or more relevant than the Cross? No, and that is not a rhetorical question. Only the Cross brings to us a righteousness that we don't deserve.

Jesus describes our lives as Christians in this way: we believers are like wheat growing among the tares or weeds. Although saved, we live in a fallen and, yes, dying world. Darkness is all around us. But God purposefully chooses not to tear out the weeds while we're growing. He will dispose of them in due time. Jesus explains His parable with these words:

"The one who sows the good seed is the Son of Man [Jesus]. *38 The field is the world, and the good seed is the sons of the kingdom. The weeds are the sons of the evil one, 39 and the enemy who sowed them is the devil. The harvest is the end of the age, and the reapers are angels. 40 Just as the weeds are gathered and burned with fire, so will it be at the end of the age. 41 The Son of Man will send his angels, and they will gather out of his kingdom all causes of sin and all law-breakers, 42 and throw them into the fiery furnace. In that place there will be weeping and gnashing of teeth. 43 Then the righteous will shine like the sun in the kingdom of their Father. He who has ears, let him hear.* Matthew 13:37-43.

I don't know about you, but I would like to be a shining example. But not for my own sake. I want to be a shining example of God's grace, mercy, and love. That doesn't mean I turn a blind eye to sin. God calls me to shine my light (His Light) on sin.

There's a lot of sin that needs to be exposed; in my life and yours - we are to be transparent and godly in what we say and do. There's also the sin of the society and world around us. You name it: pornography, abortion, ungodly sexuality, human trafficking, etc.

Thankfully, when the Light puts aside some of that debris of sin, the Cross becomes more visible. That's what we're truly after. Each of us needs to go to the Cross because that's the only place where we'll truly find the Light of God.

One final thought as we close, because this has been troubling me, and I want you to really think about it and even try it: Darkness is ALWAYS defeated and pushed back by Light. If you have a completely dark room, it only takes ONE candle or one dimly lit bulb to cast Light into it. On the other hand, for Light to be defeated, it must purposely extinguish itself; it has to allow Darkness to overcome it. That's the battle and the choice each of us faces. Light wins just because of what it is, Light, or Darkness wins because Light has allowed itself to be extinguished.

Finding Joy: Philippians, Shine

Verses: Philippians 2:12 – 18, Matthew 5:16; 13:37-43

Key Questions:

What does it mean to "work out your salvation with fear & trembling"?

What is the purpose of the Christian being "shiny"?

Is it works or faith?:

How do we bring "light" into the world?

Purposes of "light" in our lives:

1.

2.

3.

What distinguishes "light" from "darkness"?

"Light" can equal:

Homework: You are in control of your own dimmer switch. Are you turning it up or down?

Finding Joy: a Few Good Friends

An age old question is this: what constitutes being a "friend"?

As an over-50-year-old male, I've seen friends come and go. The ones who have stayed, I consider long-term friends. We can be separated due to jobs, family, and even distance. When we do connect, it's like there was only a five-minute pause in the conversation.

Now, I'm not talking about my wife. Barbara was someone very special and irreplaceable. My wife and I were knit together by God to form the nucleus of our family. Jesus is supposed to be the center of this very special relationship. When it comes under fire from external or internal forces, whatever they may be, we are to cling to our Savior first. Even when the going gets tough, we still know how the other thinks. In hard times - even between the two of us - I would never want to be joined with anyone else for a lifetime.

But then there are our friends. Both Barbara and I had, and have, our close friends, and intimate friends (female for her, male for me), whom we also depend on. These friends are essential, even for our survival.

Acquaintances are one thing, we need them too, but friends, true friends, are vital. They are vital in our work, our play or recreation, and even in our ministry that God has called us to. True friends are those men or women who not only know us really well, but are also "privileged" to call us on our foibles. We have given them, because of our friendship, the right to pull us aside or pick up the phone and say, "Hey, you're out of line about..." These folks are also the ones who know how to tend to our deepest needs without saying a word. Their presence is oftentimes all we need. A cup of coffee. A smile. A handshake or hug. Those are relationships that God created all of us for, right? And after all, God is a God of relationships, isn't He?

In Philippians 2:19-30, Paul writes about 2 very important friends in his ministry and outreach to the gentile world, and their importance not only to the message but also to him personally. Out of all of Paul's letters or epistles, this is one relatively extended passage that he dedicates to 2 friends. Here's what Paul writes:

[19] I hope in the Lord Jesus to send Timothy to you soon, so that I too may be cheered by news of you. [20] For I have no one like him, who will be genuinely concerned for your welfare. [21] For they all seek their own interests, not those of Jesus Christ. [22] But you know Timothy's proven worth, how as a son with a father he has served with me in the gospel. [23] I hope therefore to send him just as soon as I see how it will go with me, [24] and I trust in the Lord that shortly I myself will come also.

[25] I have thought it necessary to send to you Epaphroditus my brother and fellow worker and fellow soldier, and your messenger and minister to my need, [26] for he has been longing for you all and has been distressed because you heard that he was ill. [27] Indeed he was ill, near to death. But God had mercy on him, and not only on him but on me also, lest I should have sorrow upon sorrow. [28] I am the more eager to send him, therefore, that you may rejoice at seeing him again, and that I may be less anxious. [29] So receive him in the Lord with all joy, and honor such men, [30] for he nearly died for the work of Christ, risking his life to complete what was lacking in your service to me.

Timothy and Epaphroditus are two of Paul's closest friends in his ministry. Of the two, we know more about Timothy. Timothy was Paul's "son" in Christ. Paul mentored him and, over time, helped him become a strong, solid leader in the Church. The books of 1 and 2 Timothy are more than letters of instruction. They are letters from a loving and doting father to a son who has become a man. In his closing passages to Timothy, Paul pours out his heart while also offering great wisdom on how Timothy should conduct his own life. We know a fair amount about Timothy.

Epaphroditus, not so much. This man is mentioned only in this short chapter and again in Philippians chapter 4. He was a Philippian. He brought gifts to Paul from Philippi, and Paul would send him back bearing gifts of ministry and this letter.

Friends. We can't live without them. They are not to be taken for granted. Friends are true gifts from God. None of us was meant to do anything alone - especially ministry and God's Work.

Come to think of it, from Genesis 1:1 to Revelation 22:21, God never works alone. We've already said that God is a God of relationship. The Trinity of Father, Son, and Holy Spirit is always working for the ultimate Plan of the Godhead. Each has its "individual strength" and purpose. One is not subject, per se, to the other.

We see the Father working together with the Son and the Holy Spirit in the Creation of the universe. In six days, they brought everything that we see and cannot see into being. By mutual accord, they chose to create humankind in their image. After the Flood, at the Tower of Babel, they would come down together and confuse the common language. We continue to work as a team.

That's how God wants us to work in His Plan: a central core of people, friends, working toward accomplishing God's Plan. We see it throughout Scripture. In the beginning, it was a man and his wife or children, plus God, doing the work. Noah and his sons, Abraham and Sarah, Moses with Miriam and Aaron, and his father-in-law Jethro, David and his mighty men, Daniel and Shadrach, Meshach, and Abednego.

There was always a "lead" guy, along with a couple of friends and close confidants. Even Jesus worked that way. Jesus was the "lead" guy, but He had Peter, John, and James with Him. Jesus was modeling good, effective ministry.

Why do we need people to help us in ministry? Because we can't do it alone. God may be able to do it "alone," but we certainly can't. Think of what the Bible teaches us in the very basics: [9]*Two are better than one, because they have a good reward for their toil.* [10] *For if they fall, one will lift up his fellow. But woe to him who is alone when he falls and has not another to lift him up!* Ecclesiastes 4:9-10. We need one another not only in life, but in ministry.

Whether we like it or not, we as individuals do not have everything needed for effective ministry. No one does. I don't care how good a pastor, counselor, Sunday school teacher, or youth worker you are or may think you are, ministry in God's Plan requires that we have a couple of good friends to be effective. We need others to provide us with Godly counsel, to offer words of encouragement, or to aid us in physical labor. We need close friends and confidants to pray with us and for us as we do God's Work. And these men and women are there to make a difference in our lives.

Let me tell you briefly about three of my close friends in ministry. I'll use their first names. These men mean a lot to me. They've seen me (like Timothy and Epaphroditus saw Paul), in and through good times and bad. They supported me when I needed help. They admonished me when I needed some firm but loving reminding of my place. Most importantly, they prayed for me and loved me for who I am.

The first friend I mention is Bob (his real name). Bob was, and still is to a certain degree, one of my mentors. When I started teaching adult Sunday school 30 years ago, I chose Bob to teach with. I was very inexperienced; he, on the other hand, had been a teacher and management consultant for years. As we prepared our lessons week after week, we would refine them. We would keep each other on task during lesson time. He helped me hone my presentations; I would make sure that he kept his whit in line... We were a team. I am a better teacher today because of him. In my opinion, although a little sharp around the edges, Bob's a great person to have in a church, teaching teachers (lay people) how to teach. In a way, I was his Timothy.

My next two friends are Charlie and Len. Although we may not teach together as a tagteam (he has substituted for me a few times over the years), they are close friends in ministry. We serve together on our church's Adult Bible Fellowship committee. Both Charlie and Len are "task" guys. They're in "IT" or information technology. They know how to get things done. Me? I'm the idea guy. I don't necessarily know how to get it done, but I know in my mind's eye what it's supposed to look like. These two often get the first whack at critiquing many Study Series lessons and posts. They reel me in when I start getting too "out there" or help me hone an idea to make it more understandable. Charlie is definitely more concrete and linear in his thinking pattern than I will ever be, and I thank God for that. Len is a solid teacher of God's Word and Doctrine. When I have a spiritual burden, I know I can confide in either of these men and trust that they will lift my needs before God's throne of grace early in the morning (they're up way earlier than I ever would normally consider).

Bob, Charlie, and Len are just three of a cadre of men and women who are true friends in ministry. I don't know what I would or could do without God's providing them. What I do know is that without God providing Himself through the lives of others, I wouldn't have a ministry. It's not the biggest or best. It's not the snazziest, but it's what God has called me to do in this time and in this place. And for that - as well as for Bob, Charlie, and Len - I am eternally thankful. Friends, Godly and praying friends, are a very good thing in your ministry.

Friends are there to support you or help you. Friends are there to provide the talents you may not have been blessed with. Friends are there to check you when you may be going out of bounds. Friends are there to lift you when you're down and losing hope. Friends are there to pray for you, your family, and your personal needs. Friends are there to help you when you lock yourself out of your house, and a family member is hours away from letting you back in. Friends laugh with you and cry with you. Friends sometimes sit by your side and don't say a word, but they're there. I'm glad I don't have many fair-weather friends. All of them are honest and true. You can't get much better than that.

My dad died back in 1993. His name was Chris, not Christopher, just Chris. He was a faithful husband and father as well as a reasonably good businessman. He was well-liked by friends and respected by competitors. At his wake and funeral, many came to honor and remember him. He didn't have an easy life: brought up during the Great Depression, served in World War II in the South Pacific as a medic helping clean up after the battle at Guadalcanal. He married my mother in his late 30's, became a first-time father at age 40 with me. My dad always smiled.

As a businessman, he knew success and defeat. We enjoyed a comfortable prosperity, then lost much of it in a business bankruptcy. We would regroup as a family and start again, along with a few close friends for moral support. Only a few years later, just after my wife and I had adopted our first child, our daughter, my dad was diagnosed with terminal abdominal cancer with six months to live. Instead, God chose to give him about four and a half years. Yes, he had his family around him, but he always had his friends. Especially in his final months and weeks, they (his closest friends) would regularly visit or take him to lunch or breakfast.

Soon after his death, while cleaning out his desk (he never really retired), I happened to find a little self-testimonial he gave at his retirement from the local Rotary Club. I still pick it up and read it from time to time. His advice to his friends and compadres: always have and cultivate a few good friends. Have a younger friend you can mentor, and an older friend (same age group or generation) who understands your struggles.

I can't wait to see him again on the other side in Glory.

Like Moses, I think God wants us to speak and be with Him as a friend. And God has also created us for each other. Let us not only love our friends, but let us acknowledge them publicly. Let's cheer them on as they cheer us on. Let's come alongside our friends in this Great Ministry, this Great Commission, as they come alongside us, holding each other up in love, prayer, honor, and affection.

I think Paul sums it up pretty well in 1 Thessalonians 5:11. It's worth repeating: "*Therefore encourage one another and build one another up, just as you are doing.*"

And to you all I say be blessed, and be a blessing.

Finding Joy: Philippians, a Few Good Friends

Verses: Philippians 2:19 – 30; Ecclesiastes 4:9; 1 Thessalonians 5:11

Key Questions:

Why do we need friends in ministry?

Who is a friend in the ministry God gave you?

Who is Timothy:

Who is Epaphroditus:

Name & reflect on two Friends (not including your spouse) in your ministry:

1.

2.

Homework: Publicly acknowledge a friend or co-worker in the ministry that God has given you.

Finding Joy: the Right Credentials

Paul's epistle or letter to the Philippians is a book filled with life lessons.

Specifically, it teaches all of us believers in Christ Jesus how to live "in" this world, but not to be "of" it. It's amazing how two little words can make a huge difference in the context of a thought or sentence. In Philippians chapter two, we go from being "stars" shining as an example of Christ to chapter three, where Paul looks around at himself and sees nothing but rubbish.

This is an amazing dichotomy of the Christian faith, isn't it? There always seem to be contrasting ideas about what is normal in the world and its belief systems versus those of God. God has an entirely upside-down (and seemingly counterintuitive) economy for accomplishing His plans and purposes.

God uses the weak to show His strength. God makes us whole when we are completely broken. Light is "highlighted" when things or circumstances seem their darkest. Losers are actually winners in the long run of life. To live more abundantly, we have to die. All of this is confounding to the natural world, but not to God and hopefully not to us believers.

Following is what the Holy Spirit wrote to us through Paul in Philippians chapter three:

Finally, my brothers, rejoice in the Lord. To write the same things to you is no trouble to me and is safe for you.

2 Look out for the dogs, look out for the evildoers, look out for those who mutilate the flesh.
3 For we are the circumcision, who worship by the Spirit of God and glory in Christ Jesus and
put no confidence in the flesh— 4 though I myself have reason for confidence in the flesh
also. If anyone else thinks he has reason for confidence in the flesh, I have more:
5 circumcised on the eighth day, of the people of Israel, of the tribe of Benjamin, a Hebrew of
Hebrews; as to the law, a Pharisee; 6 as to zeal, a persecutor of the church; as to
righteousness under the law, blameless. 7 But whatever gain I had, I counted as loss for the

sake of Christ. [8] Indeed, I count everything as loss because of the surpassing worth of knowing Christ Jesus my Lord. For his sake I have suffered the loss of all things and count them as rubbish, in order that I may gain Christ [9] and be found in him, not having a righteousness of my own that comes from the law, but that which comes through faith in Christ, the righteousness from God that depends on faith— [10] that I may know him and the power of his resurrection, and may share his sufferings, becoming like him in his death, [11] that by any means possible I may attain the resurrection from the dead. Philippians 3:1-11

We'll go through this passage verse by verse.

Paul starts on a high note: "Rejoice in the Lord!" No matter what, rejoice. I originally wrote this lesson on Thanksgiving morning. The house was still and quiet. I just finished putting the stuffed turkey in the oven and figure that I have about two hours before the rustling of bodies. It's been a hard couple of weeks with some family and teenager issues, but you know what? God is still in control. He's on His throne. He holds all of my problems in His hands. My daughter and grandson were with us. A friend was visiting from out of town. My mom came by for lunch. The sun is rising on a crisp November morning. I have the privilege of writing another lesson about living the Christian life. God is good.

And I will rejoice! I can honestly write as Paul did, "*It is no trouble for me to write the same things to you again*". Teaching God's Word and principles is a joy. Those of us who have been called to teach, preach, and reach people with His Word find that this is not work. Many Bible lessons are taught over and over again because each of us is going through a different struggle at a different time in a different place, and God often begins teaching with His teachers. Where we once read a particular verse two weeks ago and glossed over it, a different yet similar verse at the other end of the Bible now jumps out and grabs us. God's Word is active; it is living. It is Life!

That is a really good reason to rejoice. And as we remember, re-read, and rejoice, we see and understand that God's Word stands there as a safeguard for our lives.

Paul then reminds us again of who we are as Christians. We are the circumcised. Whether male or female, when we accept Jesus Christ and His atoning death on the cross as our salvation by faith alone, God circumcises our hearts. We are not just circumcised physically, we are circumcised spiritually. God cuts out the old, sinful nature and replaces it with a new, godly nature.

In time, we will be conformed to the image of Jesus Himself. In another chapter, we saw that our salvation is to be worked out with fear and trembling. The Christian life is a journey. Dying to self is a process. For some (like me), there are parts of my sinful nature that want to hold on to and live. Like the bittersweet root growing in my flower beds around my house, which has to be constantly pulled out and killed, so too the annoying vestiges of sin that hound me and continually vex me; I have to keep pulling them out and placing them before God for my ultimate healing.

Legalists or legalism (religion), those *"who mutilate the flesh"* only want us to live by a new set of rules. We become human doings following rules and regulations rather than simply living a life according God's purposes and God's Plan. Rather than seeking after God, we seek to live a life that turns out to be just another hamster wheel. God wants us to be liberated from any and all worldly hamster wheels. In order to do that, we are to actively seek Him. As we actively seek Him in daily and regular times of prayer and reading His Word, we end up being with God. We are gradually transformed from human doings to human beings. We come to an inner and intimate knowledge *of* God rather than simply knowing *about* God.

Then Paul starts with a little tongue in cheek boasting of his earthly position. Notice verses 4 through 6:

[4] though I myself have reason for confidence in the flesh also. If anyone else thinks he has reason for confidence in the flesh, I have more: [5] circumcised on the eighth day, of the people of Israel, of the tribe of Benjamin, a Hebrew of Hebrews; as to the law, a Pharisee; [6] as to zeal, a persecutor of the church; as to righteousness under the law, blameless.

If anyone could boast about his piety, it was Paul. From a Jewish and religious point of view, he had almost reached the pinnacle. He was born into the right family, of the right tribe, within Jewish society. He followed the Law as he understood it. His faulty understanding led Paul to have a misdirected zeal to "protect" the Law, as it were, and therefore to persecute the fledgling Church. His righteousness was not Godly as it turned out. It was self-righteous and, therefore, in the end, self-aggrandizing. Paul wasn't building up the Truths of God as much as he was building up his own self-righteousness and those of the reigning priesthood.

They (the Jewish authorities, including Paul - previously known as Saul) had the Scriptures and read them each day, but something was missing. They understood the letter of the Law but not its eternal Spirit. They saw rule after rule rather than an all-encompassing story that spoke of God's mercy, grace, and sovereignty as He guided all of humanity to that moment when God Himself would reconcile the natural to the Divine. Instead of living in Godly liberty, people like Saul placed more and more chains on themselves and fellow followers of the Law.

Paul, like many of us, had or has credentials. When asked by whichever governing authority he acted, he could "show" his credentials. We do similarly. Each of us was brought up in a particular town and attended a particular school. We did this or that. Many of us have alphabet soup after our names listed on our business or calling cards that tells others of our credentials. Sometimes, credentials are meant to impress others with our accomplishments, whether academic or professional, especially those who we would consider important in our respective spheres of influence. To the average person, credentials mean little if anything. We rely on our earthly credentials rather than the only credential that God recognizes: the blood of Jesus Christ covering our (my) sins. We judge one another by these credentials rather than how God sees us: His friend, His child of the Kingdom, and His ambassador to the world.

And now Paul sees the Truth. As God revealed Himself to Paul, He purposefully reveals Himself to all of us, to each of us. We come individually to Him. There is no corporate salvation. Just because you belong to or are a part of one denomination or another doesn't justify you before God. Paul now understands the *"filthy rags"* he has up to this point, clothed himself in. God had opened not only Paul's eyes, but his heart and mind to the Truth of who he was and now Whose he is.

Notice what the apostle writes in verses 7 through 8. Three times he writes the word "loss". He has come to realize that earthly gain (credentials) is a heavenly loss compared to God.

I'm not entirely sure, but I think Paul, upon seeing God for Who He is, was completely pummeled by that fact. We have each had a similar time in our lives when, as individuals, we finally come to an understanding of our maggot-sized lives, compared to the utter Majesty, Beauty, Grace, and Sovereignty of God, and we are humbled. Every piece of our lives that we have tried to construct to make ourselves look good in the eyes of the world (other people, who actually don't really care), we now understand as a supreme loss.

In fact, Paul puts it very well when he writes that it is all "RUBBISH" (actually quite a bit more graphic in the original Greek text). That's right, rubbish. And here comes the dichotomy of God's economy: God uses rubbish - the junk in our lives and this world - to display His majesty and bring Glory to Himself.

Just think about that. That's amazing!

Knowing God through Jesus Christ is the only thing that matters in this life. Everything else is rubbish. Paul's righteousness (like yours and mine) is self-righteous. Christ is the only thing that matters. In fact, Christ and the Cross are always central to Paul's letters. Just go back and read this letter to the Philippian church. Each passage in the chapters makes a point, focusing on Christ and the Cross, then pans out into a tangible, real-life application.

Jesus Christ and His Cross are all that truly matter to this world. Everything else is rubbish. Look again at verses 8 and 9:

[8] Indeed, I count everything as loss because of the surpassing worth of knowing Christ Jesus my Lord. For his sake I have suffered the loss of all things and count them as rubbish, in order that I may gain Christ [9] and be found in him, not having a righteousness of my own that comes from the law, but that which comes through faith in Christ, the righteousness from God that depends on faith

Knowing Jesus Christ is knowing God. Not simply knowing God, but intimately knowing God is all that matters. When we know God (keep in mind that we will never know Him completely), we are complete. God provides us with credentials that, I dare say, even the angels in heaven are envious of. Angels cannot be redeemed. Only we humans carry that distinction. We remember that we men and women are created in God's image and likeness, not the angels or anything else in all of Creation. Jesus came to die and provide eternal life to humankind, not to angels.

And so we have two takeaways from this passage to apply to our lives: One: So what? And Two: At the foot of the Cross, we are all equals.

So what about "so what?" We have credentials in this life. When a potential employee comes to me for a job and tells me that they have graduated from this school or that, or worked here or there, I frankly don't really care. What I do care about is the real person inside. What are they made of? What makes them "tick"? Where do they find their fulfillment in life? What's their passion?

That's what I want to know. At that point, we can have a relationship. I know they can perform certain tasks; those are the qualifications we should be interested in. The specifics of the job - whatever it is - can be taught to almost anyone who has a willing spirit and attitude.

Even when it comes to teaching, preaching, or working out God's Word.

Unless you have a passion to live His Word out in this life and direct others to the Cross, you can have read the Word, but is has it become a part of your life? As Dr. Howard Hendricks puts it, “You've gotten into the Bible, but has the Bible gotten into you?” So what if you've read the Bible ten times, are you (am I) living it to God's glory? Are you being transformed into the image of Christ? Is your life so shining as to attract others to the Gospel of God and to Salvation? Those are the only things that matter.

Finally, it's all about the Cross. The Cross of Jesus Christ is the great equalizer of all men and women in this universe. We come as individuals. We come alone to the foot of the Cross seeking God's grace and forgiveness for sin so that we (I) may have fellowship with Him. Yes, someone may lead us there, but we come alone, responsible for our own lives, drawn by God Himself.

The Cross of Christ doesn't care whether we are rich or poor, black or white, or whatever color God designed us as. The Cross doesn't care whether we are young or old, male or female, whole or disabled, slave or free.

The Cross of Christ does care that we come. God wants us reconciled to Him. By His Grace and Mercy, God has provided a way - ONE way - of Salvation and everlasting life and fellowship with Him: the Cross of Jesus. Let's take our new, God-given credentials and show them to the world. They are the only ones that matter.

Finding Joy: Philippians, the Right Credentials

Verses: Philippians 3:1 - 11

Key Questions:

What are your credentials for Ministry?

What is “rubbish”?

Of the world:

In the world:

How are these 2 ideas contrasted?

Through the verses:

What were Paul’s credentials?

Two takeaways:

1.

2.

Homework: Think about how the credentials God has given you should be presented.

Finding Joy: Pressing On

Life is often described as a series of "mountain top" experiences.

When you think about it, that makes sense and is an appropriate visual of life.

We travel up and down the mountains (perhaps mountain range is better) of our lives. Sometimes the paths are well-traveled; we follow where others have trodden. Sometimes the paths are rocky and tricky; we have to watch ourselves along the way. Other times, there is no trail or path; we're blazing it for the first time. We expend time and energy as we struggle toward the peak. On our way up, we really don't have a good idea of what lies ahead, but we can see where we've been. As we reach the peak, there is a sense of accomplishment and relief; we have made it (at least to this point), and we can see more of the journey ahead. Sometimes, we can even rest on that peak.

Going up is arduous, but on our way down, the trip can be just as tough. We may be heading "downhill", but we still have to watch the path. We could slip and slide, and, just because it's "easier," we may not take as much care with our steps.

As we progress from peak to valley to the next peak, we move toward our goal. We may remember the "mountain top" experiences, but we tend to forget the drudgery of the journey's ups and downs. And yet we press on toward our goal. Our goal - the finish line, if you will - is our focus. We don't linger or live in the past; we look to our goal.

This is where the apostle Paul is as we come to Philippians chapter 3. Paul writes:

[12] Not that I have already obtained this or am already perfect, but I press on to make it my
own, because Christ Jesus has made me his own. [13] Brothers, I do not consider that I have
made it my own. But one thing I do: forgetting what lies behind and straining forward to
what lies ahead, [14] I press on toward the goal for the prize of the upward call of God in Christ
Jesus. [15] Let those of us who are mature think this way, and if in anything you think
otherwise, God will reveal that also to you. [16] Only let us hold true to what we have attained.

[17] Brothers, join in imitating me, and keep your eyes on those who walk according to the example you have in us. [18] For many, of whom I have often told you and now tell you even with tears, walk as enemies of the cross of Christ. [19] Their end is destruction, their god is their belly, and they glory in their shame, with minds set on earthly things. [20] But our citizenship is in heaven, and from it we await a Savior, the Lord Jesus Christ, [21] who will transform our lowly body to be like his glorious body, by the power that enables him even to subject all things to himself.

Therefore, my brothers, whom I love and long for, my joy and crown, stand firm thus in the Lord, my beloved. Philippians 3:12 - 4:1.

This passage is, in a way, a continuation of the previous section. Paul continues his thoughts and actually expands on them. We begin to answer the "so what?" question. Now that we have these Divine Credentials, what do we do with them? How do we actively participate in God's Kingdom now and in the future? Paul realizes that this Christian life - using the racing metaphor - is not a sprint or dash, it is a marathon and a lifelong marathon at that. He knows that life is a series of mountains and valleys, verdant fields and rocky crags, deserts and babbling brooks. All of those make our journey interesting, challenging, and fulfilling. And as we progress, God further develops (or even qualifies) our credentials.

In this passage, we see four points that Paul - writing by inspiration of the Holy Spirit - wishes to bring out:

1. Understanding who and Whose we are,
2. Accepting that fact,
3. Understanding the nature of the world and the people around us,
4. And our continuing relationship with our fellow brothers and sisters in the Lord.

This is not the first time that Paul uses racing or competitive imagery in his epistles. Review 2 Corinthians, Galatians, Ephesians (as quoted in Acts 20), and 2 Timothy. This imagery is something we can all relate to. We don't need to be athletic or enjoy sports. Paul - as do many of us - understands that life itself is a competition, and regardless of the particular race, challenge, or competition, we are to press on until we finish and participate as best we possibly can, knowing that we are never alone in our competition. As we proceed, we'll look at some of those passages as they are appropriate.

But let's get back to this passage: Philippians 3:12-4:1.

The first point I believe Paul is making as he develops this idea of Divine Credentials is that, as we participate in God's Kingdom, we must remember and understand who and whose we are. Paul knows that he's in a race. More importantly, he knows beyond a shadow of doubt that he is not a "perfect" runner. He hasn't yet attained the prize of God's Glory and being in His Heavenly Presence, but he knows that he'll get there in God's timing. God is in complete control of the race that Paul is running; and it is God's race, not Paul's. When we understand that distinction, the race is, I believe, a bit easier. He (as well as you and I) are racing under rules that are completely fair and honest. The time keeping is just. There will be no "photo finish". No one is given a head start or special rules to work with. No one is helped (per se) and likewise, no one is hindered.

Notice what Paul writes:

I press on to make it my own, because Christ Jesus has made me his own. That's right, JESUS took hold of Paul. Paul was the one chasing down and arresting Christians. Paul wanted nothing to do with Jesus. But Jesus - God - wanted everything to do with Paul.

Think about that fact in your own life. Were you really seeking after God and all of His ways? Some of us were like Jonah, who, although he revered God, wanted nothing to do with the great mission he had been assigned. Some of us were on the broad way to hell with all of its glitz and flashing lights and wild living. Others of us were content in our "religion" or religiosity. It was indeed God who came and took hold of us as individuals. God was the one who did the saving. We had nothing to do with our salvation except to believe in the finished work of Jesus Christ on the Cross and accept His death as payment for our sins and His resurrection as a guarantee of eternal life. God did and provided everything else, including leading us to Himself.

When God takes hold of us, I am, you are, we are His. Nothing can snatch us away from His firm and loving grip. It is amazing the lengths that God will go to keep us in His will. We were, and are, called according to His purposes, not ours. God has a plan for each of His children. The individual plans He has for each of us are not identical in scope or tactics, but the goal is the same: to bring to fruition the Kingdom of God.

And yet, we are not yet complete, which brings us to Paul's second point: accepting that fact. The fact of the matter is, we are Christ's; we belong to Him. We are not only His ambassadors, but His children and therefore heirs to His Kingdom. We are to take on our new roles with gusto and along with our new credentials. God is proud of us, and we need to be proud of Him.

So what does Paul remind us to do? We are to forget what is behind (our past, pre-Christian life) and strain toward what is ahead. We need to forget what is behind because that is the "old self" or the "old nature". If you are struggling with your identity in Christ, remember these verses:

[16] *From now on, therefore, we regard no one according to the flesh. Even though we once regarded Christ according to the flesh, we regard him thus no longer.* [17] *Therefore, if anyone is in Christ, he is a new creation. The old has passed away; behold, the new has come.* [18] *All this is from God, who through Christ reconciled us to himself and gave us the ministry of reconciliation;* 2 Corinthians 5:16-18.

When we accept Jesus Christ as our Lord and Savior, we become new creations. We're not "like" something new; we ARE new! Accept that fact.

Our individual thoughts and attitudes about God and Who He is ultimately the most important thoughts we can have on any given day. The great 20th-century theologian A. W.

Tozer wrote in his book "The Knowledge of the Holy": *"What comes to your mind when you think about God is the most important thing about you...".*

That, brothers and sisters in Christ, is a paradigm shift of being in this world but not of it. Our goal is Heaven and to hear the words "well done, good and faithful servant".

The past is exactly that: the past. It is behind us. It may occasionally nag us because of the consequences we may have to suffer, but it is still the past. The devil knows that fact all too well and seeks to trap every one of God's anointed for the purpose of tripping us up or taking us out of God's race. But we are to stay in the race. We - every man or woman who has ever trusted Jesus as their personal Savior - will finish the race and achieve our Heavenly reward. We are to live up to *"what we have* [already] *attained"* - verse sixteen. And that's a fact.

Third, the world is what it is. The world is natural. It is and has been corrupted and sinful. We may (in fact do) live in it, but it's still the world. God does love the world and gave Jesus for its salvation, but the world is still the world. And the people in the world, unless they are pursuing God, are in AND of the world.

Let's take a look at another of Paul's racing analogies found in 1 Corinthians:

[24] *Do you not know that in a race all the runners run, but only one receives the prize? So run that you may obtain it.* [25] *Every athlete exercises self-control in all things. They do it to receive a perishable wreath* [crown or prize], *but we an imperishable.* 1 Corinthians 9:24-25.

One of the great things about the Christian life is that we're all winners. We all get prizes - but don't confuse these prizes with "participation" trophies. We all get gold crowns. But we are still called to "run" a race. We are to run in such a way that our goal is First Place. We can't dog this race. We race with believers as well as unbelievers, and as Christians, we're running a different kind of race. The believer's race has God as its goal. The unbeliever's race has itself as its goal, which, in a way, almost means they are chasing their own tail. But look at the distinction Paul makes between the believer and the unbeliever, back to Philippians 3: 18 - 21.

[18] For many, of whom I have often told you and now tell you even with tears, walk as enemies of the cross of Christ. [19] Their end is destruction, their god is their belly, and they glory in their shame, with minds set on earthly things. [20] But our citizenship is in heaven, and from it we await a Savior, the Lord Jesus Christ, [21] who will transform our lowly body to be like his glorious body, by the power that enables him even to subject all things to himself.

That's a lesson unto itself! The unbeliever is an enemy. At one time, we were enemies too, but no longer. Look at the course they are racing on: the stomach or physical needs and desires, personal pride and glory, all of which are earthly issues and idols. All of these ultimately lead to or are brought to completion in *their* destiny, which is destruction and eternal separation from God in hell. We further note that the unbeliever is not "eagerly" awaiting a Savior - well, maybe one that saves them from temporal trials - and especially not one that demands control over everything and every part of every person's life. The unbeliever doesn't want any of that. Many believe that they are their own god. Their demanding, self-centered nature is their focus of achievement.

We, believers, should want all that God offers. Our destination is Heaven. Our god is God. We desire that God have all glory, honor, and power. Our mind is (better be) on God, heavenly things, and His Word. We already have a heavenly citizenship (our credentials). Christians wait expectantly for our Savior, because we know that when He does return, He will make everything new, the way He intended it to be in the first place, with brand new bodies as an eternal bonus! It can't get any better than that.

So, finally, what are we to do? We are to run a fine race along with our fellow brothers and sisters in Christ. Paul writes that we are to "stand firm" in this race. Sounds a little crazy, doesn't it? Standing firm while running? But that's how God operates.

How do we stand firm along with other believers? We hold each other up in prayer. We come alongside one another as friends in ministry (like Timothy and Epaphroditus or my friends Bob, Charlie, and Len). We are not to run our race as if "in vain," Galatians 2:2.

Furthermore, we are to help make sure that the world isn't cutting in on us. Galatians 5:7 says and asks (I like how the NIV puts it):

"You were running a good race. Who cut in on you and kept you from obeying the truth?" The world will always throw whatever it takes to distract us from our goal and our prize. We are to run, as it were, with blinders on to eliminate or at least minimize the distractions of this life. And sometimes we need to help each other adjust those blinders so that our focus is on Christ alone.

That's hard, but we have to do it; we must allow the Holy Spirit to discipline our lives. In many ways, we are our brothers' and sisters' keepers. That's what Christian love is all about, isn't it? Out of love, we keep one another from falling, and we cheer as the race progresses. I couldn't do life without any of you praying for me and coming alongside me. Each of us is the physical hands and feet and ears and eyes and kind and loving words of a Great and Holy God. We run alone, yet as a group or family. We are participants and spectators at the same time.

Let's wrap this lesson up with one of my favorite passages. We read this passage at my dad's funeral. Like Paul, he had run a good race. The road had come to an end. Paul writes to his son in the faith and friend in ministry, Timothy, his "victory speech"; they are words of encouragement:

[6] *For I am already being poured out as a drink offering, and the time of my departure has come.* [7] *I have fought the good fight, I have finished the race, I have kept the faith.* [8] *Henceforth there is laid up for me the crown of righteousness, which the Lord, the righteous judge, will award to me on that day, and not only to me but also to all who have loved his appearing.* 2 Timothy 4:6-8.

Paul may have written those words while he was in a lonely, rat-infested dungeon shortly before his death by beheading, but there is a sense of overwhelming victory in those words. Paul was not defeated. The message of the Gospel was not defeated. No, there were none of those negatives; there were only positives: there was victory and a crown. There is eternal life and fellowship with God. This is more than good news; this is great news for all who choose to put their faith in Jesus Christ!

The race is long and at times arduous. For many of us, we sometimes thought we would never arrive. But with perseverance and God's loving and guiding hand, we will make it. We'll cross the finish line.

And not only is there victory and a crown, but God Himself is there applauding Paul - and us too when the time comes. Paul would hear the words from Jesus say, *'Well done, good and faithful servant. ...Enter into the joy of your master.'* Matthew 25:23

Heaven is where we belong. That's what we were created for – to be in personal communion with the Father for eternity. Let's run our race or climb those mountains and get there. We're almost there. Press on!

Week 7 - Life Lessons: Philippians, Pressing On

Verses: Philippians 3:12 – 4:1; 1 Corinthians 9:24-25; 2 Timothy 4:7-8

Key Questions:

What is your goal or focus?

Do you know & understand your purpose in God's Plan?

Of racing & mountain tops…

What is Paul's fascination with racing?

Through the verses:

Four Points:

1.

2.

3.

4.

Victory speech:

Homework: What blinders do you need to successfully run your race?

Finding Joy: Anxiety, Depression & Restoration, Part 1

One of the most beloved passages of Scripture found in the New Testament is Philippians 4:6-7.

[6] do not be anxious about anything, but in everything by prayer and supplication with thanksgiving let your requests be made known to God. [7] And the peace of God, which surpasses all understanding, will guard your hearts and your minds in Christ Jesus.

It's a "how-to" guide for dealing with everyday problems or issues. And that's fine, but I think there's a larger issue here. Let's take a closer and longer look at not only these two verses, but also what comes before and after them. Let's get the context in order. A couple of thoughts may be conjecture, but we're going to be very close, if not on the mark.

The great apostle Paul is in prison in Rome. His epistle, or letter, to the Philippian church is intended for encouragement and instruction. That's always what a good teacher does; they instruct while also encouraging. This epistle is also typical of Paul in that he follows a structure of introduction, instruction, practical application, and, towards the end, extends personal greetings or commendations to individual people. And so, to get the full picture, we start at verse two of chapter four and learn about Euodia (pronounced u-o-dia) and Synteche (pronounced sin-tick-ee), two women in the Philippian church. There is an apparent problem, and Paul needs to address it. And as he addresses the situation, I believe greater truths begin to spill forth.

Before we go forward, let me first confess to you, dear readers, that I personally deal with bouts of depression. I have for most of my adult life. Thankfully, I don't need to be medicated, but I do need to check myself when I see myself slipping. Depression is a debilitating problem. It can not only sap your strength, but it can also lead to broken personal relationships and ultimately, a broken or "unhealthy" relationship with God. I may not be a professional therapist or counselor, but I see how God wants us to be whole with

Him, with our fellow human beings, and also with ourselves, based on my own personal experiences. This is the subject we'll tackle next.

In verses two and three of Philippians chapter four, we see Paul pleading with Euodia and Synteche to address their individual problem with one another. He's begging them to be reconciled.

Paul writes, [2] *I entreat Euodia and I entreat Syntyche to agree in the Lord.* [3] *Yes, I ask you also, true companion, help these women, who have labored side by side with me in the gospel together with Clement and the rest of my fellow workers, whose names are in the book of life.*

These are Christian women. They have worked with Paul in building the fledgling Philippian church. They have worked hard to proclaim and further the Gospel of Christ. Yet they are also contending with one another. Paul has heard about their personal strife, whatever it happens to be. And at this point, I believe the Holy Spirit whispers to Paul and says, "Hey, you have a teachable moment here. Use it." And so Paul takes the opportunity to lovingly teach a truth about our attitudes toward one another, our personal attitude, and how those problems and attitudes can affect everything around us.

Now the stage is set for Paul to continue. Paul knows that satan, the great deceiver, will do anything that he can to try and disrupt God's Plan. Let's face it and be brutally honest: most church problems do not have their roots in outside influences. Instead, they come from within the body. We, believers, may be saved, but all of us still have a very sinful nature. Our sanctification process doesn't end until we are - one way or the other - in God's direct presence.

Satan stirs the pot in disunity and discontent; then steps away. He reminds us of what someone said - maybe years earlier - about us or a loved one; then steps away. Soon, the otherwise outwardly "good-looking" church and its congregation are in reality a festering, just-beneath-the-surface cauldron of divisiveness and potential contempt. You can see how the Gospel will be affected.

Before Paul gets to his point, he is overtly kind, reminding the Philippians to "rejoice". Philippians is the "epistle of joy". Paul knows that when we rejoice even through our most difficult circumstances, there will be a return to Christian gentleness (grace) that is (or should be) the hallmark of the Church. It is grace that separates true Christianity from any other religious system in its power to change lives. The Philippians had done many good things for Paul and the rest of the Church, but here was a stumbling block that could affect everything in the future. Paul also knew that when we deal with sin (God deals with sin), it is a personal thing.

[6] *do not be anxious about anything, but in everything by prayer and supplication with thanksgiving let your requests be made known to God.* [7] *And the peace of God, which surpasses all understanding, will guard your hearts and your minds in Christ Jesus.* Philippians 4:6-7.

Satan knows that, to take us down, he will need to work through our minds. But God Himself will take care of this. These verses are the recipe for restoration, but we first need to understand the decay that can happen and the interpersonal problems that may develop if prayer is not engaged. Let's look at this downward spiral of anxiety and depression and its potential and real harm to ourselves and God's Church. Here in Part 1, we'll go down to the depths, then in Part 2, we'll come back up. First, we'll get SADDDR, then we'll ROR back to health. Sorry, I don't mean to be silly or sarcastic, but that's just how this has worked out! God does have a sense of humor.

We start with S, which stands for Strife and/or the Situation. The situation with Euodia and Synteche involved some strife between the two Christian women. Paul has to plead with them and the other believers in the Philippian church. They must come together to solve whatever the situation is. We can assume that it's not a trifling issue. For Paul to hear about it in Rome and then respond to it, though veiled, it had to have been significant.

Think about yourself. Someone, anyone, does something "to you". It could have been major. It could have been something insignificant. It could have even been silly. Depending on our perception, it could and sometimes does turn into something huge. It festers and grows. Ant hills become the Rocky Mountains or the Himalayas. We begin to think about it more and more. Some of us will choose to ignore the "crime" committed against us, others will pick at it until seemingly every moment is spent dealing with this, this mess.

But how did this, how could this happen in a church of all places? As we mentioned already, we're dealing with people, their personalities, and their foibles: saved sinful men and women. That's our nature; although converted by the power of Christ, we will continue to wrestle with sin. Even Paul wrestled with sin (see Romans 7:14-25).

In the book of Philippians, we see little markers that Paul speaks of along the way. There is their "conduct" mentioned in Phil 1:27. Paul had to remind them to *"let your manner of life be worthy of the gospel of Christ,"*. We will naturally NOT conduct ourselves properly. We don't have to be taught to do ill; it's instinctual. We DO, however, have to be taught to act properly. Paul writes in chapter 2:3 to remind them not to be selfish and do things out of *"selfish ambition or conceit"*. We are to look out for *"the interests of others"*; verse 4.

Further in chapter 2, the Philippians (all of us Christians) are urged to continue to do good works, *"work out your own salvation"* without *" grumbling or disputing "* (verses 12 through 14). We see all of this with Euodia and Synteche. This is how we all naturally operate. It takes work to NOT operate in this fashion.

Finally, in Philippians 3:13, the church at Philippi is reminded that, to move forward, the past must be put behind them. For some, that's really hard. We want to hold onto the past. We purposely choose not to forgive and forget. And all the while, the A in SADDDDR comes to life.

A stands for Anxiety. As we pore over these situations, problems, and issues in our minds, we become anxious. And we're talking about the "bad" anxiousness or anxiety. This is the anxiety that causes us to fret or anticipate, only toward the "bad" that may happen. We become pessimistic about the prospects for resolving the problem.

So not only are we "consumed" by any wrongs done to us, but we stir ourselves up. We allow our minds to dwell on these issues, whether they are real or perceived. And of course, while we're dwelling on this stuff, other "bad" stuff happens: an unexpected bill arrives in the mail; your cell phone dies; you can't make the printer work; deer eat your favorite flowers in the garden. The list goes on and on. And we become more anxious - about everything.

What did Jesus say about worry or anxiety? He was quite succinct about it. We read in Matthew 6:25-27:

25 "Therefore I tell you, do not be anxious about your life, what you will eat or what you will drink, nor about your body, what you will put on. Is not life more than food, and the body more than clothing? 26 Look at the birds of the air: they neither sow nor reap nor gather into barns, and yet your heavenly Father feeds them. Are you not of more value than they? 27 And which of you by being anxious can add a single hour to his span of life?

We have allowed "garbage" into our lives. And as garbage goes in, garbage comes out. We need a mental shower or a mind change. Our focus needs to be on God and Who He is and Whose we (you and I) are.

I've been there. Unfortunately, often. It's not pretty. The worst part is that because we won't or don't deal with it at the time, the anxiety does indeed get worse. Soon, it reaches the point where you don't even want to get out of bed in the morning. You're afraid the phone will ring, and even though you have caller ID, you don't want to hear it. You're happy sitting, playing solitaire, or looking at social media. But at church, when people ask, we say that everything is just "fine" (we're now lying to our brothers and sisters in Christ rather than being honest with them - we're being sinful).

Now we come to our first D: Depression. As I said, I am not a psychologist or trained professional, but I have been through this. Thankfully, I chose to seek help. I know I can't do this alone. Seeking help is not a crutch. Seeking help is one of the first steps in the restoration process. And we'll get there later. But first, we have to camp out here in the depression for just a bit.

Depression is debilitating. I'll speak for myself. When my depression deepens, I want to hide from the world. I don't want to come out of my room. It takes effort to pull back the curtains in the morning and see God's beautiful sunshine. Thankfully, God has spared me from ever needing medication. Instead, God has surrounded me with a cadre of good Christian friends - men, women, pastors, professionals - that I can call and talk to anytime. They help correct the path I may be on and redirect me.

But depression hurts. It hurts mentally. It hurts physically. It hurts emotionally. It hurts relationally, which leads to our next D.

Disagreement with others. When I am depressed, I am disagreeable. I find myself subconsciously - or even consciously - finding fault with others for no apparent reason, which is exactly where Euodia and Synteche are.

Paul is pleading with them, as individuals and as the greater Philippian church, to instead agree with one another. Differences must be set aside, and some common ground found to address the disagreement. Trust is often lost. A general undermining of the entire relationship begins to develop. As this disagreement continues there is an obvious...

Disruption in human relationships. The relationship between Euodia and Synteche has been disrupted. These *"fellow workers"* in the Gospel were now "disrupted". They couldn't - conjecture on my part - work together. Whatever work they were about to do would or could be diminished. That's a real shame.

And unfortunately, we see this all too often in the church. This person doesn't want to work with that one. Another person has an "attitude" toward them; you attach the reason. There is a lack of unity. The body of believers is slowly but surely being poisoned from the inside out. Even worse, no one, not one person, says anything. Nothing. This is a church, for goodness sake, a body of believers in Jesus Christ, the Savior of the world. Everything is "FINE". No, it's not.

Answer me this: what's so lovely about a church full of disrupted humans? No wonder the world sees us as hypocrites and no better than themselves. And now this leads to our final D.

Disruption in our relationship with God. Let me ask you a simple question (one I've asked myself): how can you say you have a "good" relationship with God if your relationship with your wife, child, or whoever is disrupted?

As I look at my own life, when my interpersonal relations are disrupted or even worse, broken, my relationship with God is fractured. My time spent reading His Word is more tedious. The song in my heart is not as joyful. My prayer time is flat or "unfruitful". This is true, right? Jesus spoke about this exact dilemma.

In Matthew 5:23-24, Jesus says,

[23] "Therefore, if you are offering your gift at the altar and there remember that your brother or sister has something against you, [24] leave your gift there in front of the altar. First go and be reconciled to them; then come and offer your gift.

And really notice what He says, "*your brother ...has something against YOU.*" YOU are (I am) the one with the problem, not the other person.

God expects us to deal with our own personal sin. To restore my fellowship with God, I have to begin by reconciling with my brother (sister). We have reached the bottom of this spiral. We're at a crossroads. Let's start looking up.

The good news is that there is Restoration. Restoration is a process. And it is a good process. Sometimes slow. Sometimes difficult, but it is a good and proper process.

The path to restoration starts with recognizing Who God is and who we are. In everything, we human beings are completely dependent upon God. That's why it's necessary to "think on these things..." When we put the Truths of God into our minds and actually trust Him, we turn the corner toward restoration. When we're in God's Word (hopefully on a daily basis), we understand whose we are. God cares so much for His children, for you and for me. He even said so,

[17] *The righteous cry out, and the Lord hears them;*
he delivers them from all their troubles.
[18] *The Lord is close to the brokenhearted*
and saves those who are crushed in spirit.
[19] *The righteous person may have many troubles,*
but the Lord delivers him from them all;
[20] *he protects all his bones,*
not one of them will be broken. Psalm 34:17-20.

Let's begin the process by turning to God for restoration and life. He's waiting.

We'll examine this process of Restoration in Part 2.

Finding Joy: Philippians, Anxiety, Depression & Restoration, Part 1

Verses: Philippians 4:2-9, 1 Corinthians 10:13,

Questions to answer:

What can bring about anxiety & disrupted relationships?

How do we bring restoration?

The Problem:

The Downward Cycle of Anxiety:

S

A

D

D

D

D

R

Homework: Meditate on & memorize 1 Corinthians 10:13 (in addition to the Philippians 4:6-9 above). Use these as “circuit breakers” for anxiety. Change what you listen to, read & watch. Remember GIGO. Garbage In, Garbage Out.

Finding Joy: Anxiety, Depression & Restoration, Part 2

According to the television commercial, "depression hurts". And so it does.

One of the beauties of God is that He wants His children to not only be happy, but whole. He wants our relationships to be whole, not only with Him but also with one another. In Philippians 4:2, we read of two ladies in the Philippian church, Euodia and Synteche, whose relationship was not whole. Heck, it was broken. And the apostle Paul, in writing to the church, pleaded with these women and the entire church to reconcile and restore the relationship.

And in this admonition, Paul is given a teaching moment: how to not only restore broken relationships, but also how to deal with anxiety and depression. In Part One, we looked at the downward spiral of anxiety and depression. We used the acronym SADDDR: Strife or Situation, Anxiety, Depression, Disruption in human relationships, Disruption in our relationship with God, and Restoration.

Let's continue with Restoration, and its process. I believe if we firmly grasp Restoration, the process of spiraling down into depression can be reversed. Again, let's read Philippians 4:6-7, which provides the foundation for the restorative process, [6]*do not be anxious about anything, but in everything by prayer and supplication with thanksgiving let your requests be made known to God.* [7]*And the peace of God, which surpasses all understanding, will guard your hearts and your minds in Christ Jesus.*

Using and following God's Word, we will hopefully understand how we can stop the downward spiral of anxiety and depression and begin an upward spiral of restoration and healing. Not only will we be healed as individuals, but healing and restoration will begin in our personal, professional, and church relationships.

Before proceeding, we need to understand another truth Paul brings out. In 1 Corinthians 10:13, he makes this statement, and it's very applicable to this entire discussion,

[13] No temptation has overtaken you except what is common to mankind. And God is faithful; he will not let you be tempted beyond what you can bear. But when you are tempted, he will also provide a way out so that you can endure it.

All of us sin. All of us are tempted to sin, regardless of whether we have been Christians for days or decades. You (I) will be tempted to sin in some way against someone else, and therefore, God. Euodia and Synteche were both tempted (we don't know exactly what), and they each succumbed to the sin that brought about strife, anxiety, disagreement, a disruption in their relationship, a potential disruption of the relationship within the entire Philippian church, and most importantly, a disruption in their personal relationships with God. Notice that Paul points out the struggle in the mind. The mind should be the place of God's intellect in our lives, but too often we (I) allow it to become the devil's playground instead. And when he plays there, he doesn't pick up after himself. Evil always prefers chaos rather than order.

Thankfully, it is God Himself who provides the ways and means of escape from sin. We may have to swallow our individual pride. We may have to make some hard choices to exit this sin or sinful path, but/and God has provided a way out.

Let's look at this restoration process. I have used it in my own life to combat anxiety and depression and begin the healing process with my interpersonal relationships. This process is not a panacea; it's not a magic formula, but God wants us reconciled to one another for His Glory and honor. And in the end, we'll be able to rejoice!

First, we need to Restore our Relationship with God. Although we are Christians, we (I) can disrupt our (my) relationship with Him. He is holy. I'm not. There are things that I have to do. Can I "stop sinning"? Frankly, that's impossible! But I can make changes to my life so that I will sin less.

In part 1, we talked briefly about GIGO; you know, garbage in, garbage out. What garbage have I put into my life, whether consciously or "unconsciously"? What am I watching on television? What am I doing or viewing online? What "jokes" do I snicker at? What kinds of music do I listen to? What am I reading? How do I talk to people? The list goes on and on. That's a lot of potential garbage going into my heart and mind. As it accumulates, it eventually spills out; *how can you who are evil say anything good? For the mouth speaks what the heart is full of.* Matthew 12:34. As Dr. Voddie Baucham used to say, "If you can't say Amen, say ouch!"

My thoughts, words, and deeds become calloused and hard. Rather than being potential "healing balms," these are various salts sprinkled on hurting wounds.

As I restore my relationship with God, I must redirect my life to His purposes, not mine. To rediscover His plans for my life, I have to know more about God. I have to commit my free time to Bible reading and study. I have to make the time to commune or be in prayer with God. If I care about my relationship with God - as with any significant relationship - I have to work at it. I may have to come to know God anew. It's not that I've lost my salvation, but because I sinned, I - not God - have disrupted this most intimate of relationships.

What can we further do to restore our relationship with God? We start in the following verses, Philippians 4:8-9, [8] *Finally, brothers, whatever is true, whatever is honorable, whatever is just, whatever is pure, whatever is lovely, whatever is commendable, if there is any excellence, if there is anything worthy of praise, think about these things.* [9] *What you have learned and received and heard and seen in me—practice these things, and the God of peace will be with you.*

Having a change of mindset is a good and proper start, but for full restoration, we have to go deeper still. Don't worry, God, writing through Paul, provides the solutions. Turn over to Paul's letter to the Colossians, right after Philippians.

Let's follow Paul's advice for good, proper Christian living. First, we need to bring "Order" to ourselves,

[5] *For though I am absent from you in body, I am present with you in spirit and delight to see how disciplined* [orderly] *you are and how firm your faith in Christ is.* Colossians 2:5. We are to be "disciplined" or "orderly". When we are disciplined or orderly, our faith in Christ is firm (that's a whole separate topic).

Second, when we are disciplined or orderly, we become [7] *rooted and built up in him, strengthened in the faith as you were taught, and overflowing with thankfulness.* Colossians 2:7.

Being orderly and disciplined helps us set aside time to be in God's Word, to pray, to keep our households and businesses in order, and to attend to other life's tasks. When I look back on the chaotic times of my life, which resulted in struggle, even to the point of not making time to commune with my Savior, it was because I slipped into "not caring" or "going with the flow". It takes work to fight back against disorder and chaos, which are natural to sin.

After becoming orderly in our lives and rooted and built up in Christ, there are things that we need to get rid of.

[8] *But now you must also rid yourselves of all such things as these: anger, rage, malice, slander, and filthy language from your lips.* [9] *Do not lie to each other, since you have taken off your old self with its practices* [10] *and have put on the new self, which is being renewed in knowledge in the image of its Creator.* Colossians 3:8-10. That's what Euodia and Synteche would have to do. How much more for you and me?

Remember that each of us is created in the image and likeness of God. Being created in the image of God, we share His communicable attributes, including His "looks," and one of those attributes is relationship. We are to live in interpersonal relationships: the vertical relationship with God and the horizontal relationship with one another.

Finally, after getting rid of stuff (not to mention remembering Whose and who we are), we have to fill the void. Leaving it empty doesn't work. The bad stuff will naturally come back.

We have to refill ourselves with new and good stuff. Continuing in Colossians chapter three, we read in verses 12 through 17:

[12] Therefore, as God's chosen people, holy and dearly loved, clothe yourselves with compassion, kindness, humility, gentleness and patience. [13] Bear with each other and forgive one another if any of you has a grievance against someone. Forgive as the Lord forgave you. [14] And over all these virtues put on love, which binds them all together in perfect unity.

[15] Let the peace of Christ rule in your hearts, since as members of one body you were called to peace. And be thankful. [16] Let the message of Christ dwell among you richly as you teach and admonish one another with all wisdom through psalms, hymns, and songs from the Spirit, singing to God with gratitude in your hearts. [17] And whatever you do, whether in word or deed, do it all in the name of the Lord Jesus, giving thanks to God the Father through him.

I don't know about you, but that's a pretty daunting "to-do" list! Thankfully, God is loving and kind. He is patient. He provides whatever I may need to heal our relationship. In performing these tasks, I am "cleaning the inside of the cup." Matthew 23:25 and Luke 11:39.

God reminds me that, as sinful and broken as I am, and more than I realize, He has loved me more than I can ever imagine.

As my Relationship with God is restored, I can begin restoring my Human Relationships. God's hand may be heavy, but His hand is covered with the velvet glove of Grace.

I love being a grandfather. And being a grandparent means that, in those early years, we have to go back to changing dirty diapers from time to time. Yup. Thought that had been put to rest a long time ago, but no. And so, that is with every human relationship. We deal with "poopy diapers". Poopy diapers must be lovingly removed and disposed of. Even though we may be "comfortable" in them - sorry for being graphic, but it's a great picture of the human condition - they stink.

Do I have broken or disrupted relationships? Yes, I do. I'm not proud of that fact, but it's true. God has called me to work on these relationships personally. And as I lean into God and His Word, He provides me with the verbal and emotional tools with which to begin the healing process. We use the tools and examples that Paul provided to the Colossians in the passage we just read. It takes work.

What I can tell you, from personal experience, is that as I put into practice those "what to do's", I can gradually restore my human relationships.

As my human relationships improve and are restored, the disagreements gradually turn into Agreements. Do we still "disagree" on certain aspects or issues? Yes. But we "agree to disagree," and the personal animosity or judgments are lessened.

My wife used to get frustrated with me about certain things - like you should be surprised! My wife was a perfectionist, and let's say that I'm not. That has caused many disagreements over the years. I have had to rethink several things I do to please her. I could stand my ground and be right, but what's the sense in going down the depression spiral again over how the toilet paper comes off the roll?

As I sought to please my wife, I came to accept certain of her idiosyncrasies. Barbara also had to agree with some of mine. It is good to be agreeable. And now that she's been gone these several years, frankly, I better understand the need to be orderly and seek to do things – anything – to the best of my ability, as she always sought to.

Do not take this as living like a doormat for someone else. We're not talking about important things (eternal things are important things). And yes, there are some parts of our thoughts and thinking and acts that are not negotiable: our relationship with God, proper dealings with substance abuse, coming to a common ground on how we discipline our kids; those types of issues or concerns.

Agreements or agreeing with others that you may be in conflict with can lead to acceptance.

Anxiety becomes Acceptance. Acceptance is a huge thing to understand. When it comes to understanding grace, acceptance is foundational. Acceptance can also be understood as humility. Do we have the humility to come forward, accept our part in the strife or situation, and ask forgiveness? Or do we want to be "right" for the sake of being right?

We are all sinners. We are all broken in some way, shape, or form. Those of us who have accepted Jesus as our personal Savior have Him as our mediator: a Mediator before the throne of God and a Mediator between us, His children. As God reshapes me and renews my mind, I gradually get used to my "new" set of eyes; eyes that see others as Jesus sees others.

Acceptance also means accepting me for who I am. It's not that I've "lowered" myself to others' levels, but I come to an acceptance and understanding that all of us stand equally before the Cross. He knows that I won't be "perfect" until He brings me home to heaven. If that's okay with God, that's okay with me.

Strife and their situations remain what they are, but they are also Opportunities to demonstrate love and grace. God loves you, me, and all that He has created. He always wants the best for our happiness and His glory. These situations of love and grace reach out to tell the unsaved and unbelieving world around us that there is something special about our Faith. Something is exciting about God's Love.

God wants us to act like His children; children of the King. We are to be attractive to the world around us. They should be banging at our doors wanting what we have. We Christians know what true love is; the world doesn't. Here's what the Apostle John said in his later years,

16 This is how we know what love is: Jesus Christ laid down His life for us. And we ought to
lay down our lives for our brothers and sisters. 17 If anyone has material possessions and sees
a brother or sister in need but has no pity on them, how can the love of God be in that
person? 18 Dear children, let us not love with words or speech but with actions and in truth.

[19] This is how we know that we belong to the truth and how we set our hearts at rest in His presence: [20] If our hearts condemn us, we know that God is greater than our hearts, and He knows everything. 1 John 3:16-20.

We love God. He loves us. We love one another. Love heals. Love protects. God's Love and Peace transcend all human understanding. Love, coupled with God's peace, guards our hearts and minds with the power of Christ.

Dear friends, as we close this lesson on Philippians 4:2-9, I ask you to seek God if there's some "cup cleaning" that needs attention. Seek out a trusted friend (preferably someone who won't necessarily agree with you) who will love you through this process. If you believe you need professional assistance, don't wait. Don't be ashamed. You're not alone. Help is there and available. Your well-being, being well, and wholeness are worth the time.

God wants you whole.

Heavenly Father, I pray for anyone who is in deep mental pain and anguish. I pray that You draw near to them and begin the healing process. If there is strife between two of Your children, may Your Spirit begin to work in their individual hearts to start the healing process and return them to a state of contentedness, relying on Your Grace. Father, we have presented our requests, with thanksgiving, knowing that You truly hear us and know our needs. Guard our hearts and minds in Christ Jesus, we pray. Amen.

Finding Joy: Philippians, Anxiety, Depression & Restoration, Part 2

Verses: Philippians 4:2-9, 1 Corinthians 10:13, Colossians 2:5-7, 3:8-10, 1 John 3:16-20

Questions to answer:

What can bring about healing & restored relationships?

What is the result of restoration?

The Solution:

The Upward Climb toward Restoration:

R

O

R

A

A

O

Homework: Continue to meditate on & memorize 1 Cor 10:13 (in addition to the Phil 4:6-9 above). Use these as "circuit breakers" for anxiety. Change what you listen to & read & watch. Remember GIGO. Garbage In, Garbage Out.

Finding Joy: Regular Maintenance

There is nothing in the universe that is getting "better" or "evolving".

Perhaps a bottle of wine, but even that - sooner or later - is going to become an expensive bottle of vinegar.

Show me one thing that is naturally improving or transforming from one (current) state to a "better" (and it has to be able to be measured quantitatively as well as qualitatively) or more complex or technologically advanced state without any direct or indirect outside aid.

I look at my desk, basement, or garage and, without help or care, they're either getting more cluttered or dirty; they're not getting cleaner. The house needs, or if it has exterior siding, the interior rooms need an occasional coat of paint or a bit of fixing up. Cars need regular servicing. Outdoor furniture corrodes or decays; even plastic becomes brittle with age. Gardens become overgrown with weeds. Many beaches need the sand replaced due to storms and normal erosion.

And we're not even talking about our bodies! The body of a fifty-something is definitely not the same as a twenty-something, regardless of exercise and good nutrition.

Literally everything around us is degrading, or "devolving" if you will, in some way, shape, or form. If we want things to "get better" or at least be maintained, someone has to perform regular, routine maintenance. If this maintenance isn't kept up, these things, including our own bodies, will fail. Just try stopping breathing, drinking water, or eating for a time and see how things work out - you will die.

Even our minds need regular maintenance! It is such an incredible shame to see once-vibrant people become stale, or sometimes just plain ornery (or, in some cases, foolish) from a lack of regular mental exercise. Not mental gymnastics, but exercise that stretches one's cognitive abilities.

Before moving on to the final passage in Philippians, I want to zero in on Philippians 4:8-9 and give it extra attention. This is one of those "got to memorize" passages in the Bible. We Christians should have this one in our top ten to regularly meditate on and even use as a daily checklist as we live life. Paul writes:

[8] Finally, brothers, whatever is true, whatever is honorable, whatever is just, whatever is pure, whatever is lovely, whatever is commendable, if there is any excellence, if there is anything worthy of praise, think about these things. [9] What you have learned and received and heard and seen in me—practice these things, and the God of peace will be with you.

Notice what Paul says, "think about these things." He doesn't say do or say (although that should be the outcome), but think. Hmm.

Some perspective.

Let's take a step back before moving forward.

When we first come to faith in Christ, we become new creations. We are transformed. The "old" man becomes "new". Unfortunately, this "new creation" is still living in its old sinful body, amongst sinful old creations in an old and sinful world. To say that this is not the ideal situation would be an understatement. Something drastic or radical must take place. God has done the heavy lifting of saving us from our sins, but He requires that we take part - and I would go so far as to say at least partial ownership - of the continued sanctification and transformation processes.

And where does that transformation process take place? The transformation takes place in the mind. In our thoughts, even to the point of our subconscious, while we sleep. Our minds are always active and processing.

As the Holy Spirit transforms us, there must be renewal. To fully "be" with God (in our worship and in our lives), we must put on our new selves and become Christ-like. Not only

So what is a noble thought? Noble thoughts are similar in that they are majestic, powerful, and sweeping. Noble thoughts capture our imagination and provide vision for great and godly pursuits. Noble thoughts not only spur our minds to do what is right, but also cause us to want to include others. Glory is shared between men and women. Glory is given to God.

"Whatever is just [right]." Righteous thoughts are good and powerful thoughts. Righteous thoughts are often very other-centered; they are self-sacrificial. Right thoughts bring healing to otherwise hurtful situations. God is righteous. *"Lord, the God of Israel, you are righteous [just]!"* Ezra 9:15.

From time to time, I've had to tell my kids (which reminds me...) to apologize to someone else, even if the act was completely unintentional and carried no malice. Sometimes we need to help someone who may be perfectly capable of doing something on their own, but the act of kindness is appreciated (or not). We think about these things and then actually do them because, as I've told them, "it's the right thing to do." Now, I need to remember to follow through more often myself!

"Whatever is pure." As we get older - some people call it maturity - we sometimes lose a sense of what is pure; the world (especially in 21st-century Western culture) has, in a way, desensitized us to impurity. Purity lacks guile. There's no agenda. A pure thought has nothing attached to it that might cause it to become dirty. I don't fully understand why people tell "off-color" or "dirty" jokes, or why these "jokes" are even called "adult humor". Their thoughts and words are crass and rude. God is not crass or rude; He is pure. *"Your eyes are too pure to look on evil."* Habakkuk 1:13.

Having had my three-year-old grandson live with us for a while, and his daddy being deployed internationally, has on more than one occasion reminded me that my speech to him, or even around him, has to be pure and right, even to the point of being "holy". Like it or not, he has repeated certain of my outbursts and phrases that aren't pure. What is he learning from me as I speak? We remember what Jesus said: *"Out of the abundance of the heart, the mouth speaks."* (Matthew 12:34)

If that's how we're speaking, then our hearts have stored up too much impurity that the mind has allowed in - both consciously and unconsciously - through any of our sensory gates.

"Whatever is lovely." Thinking about lovely things is uplifting to me. It's like looking out on a beautiful garden in full bloom or one of the natural wonders that God has blessed us with. Looking at, viewing, and thinking about lovely things refreshes and brings peace to my mind. God is lovely. *"How lovely is your dwelling place, Lord Almighty!"* Psalm 84:1.

I don't know about you, but when I am thinking of pure and lovely thoughts, I tend to be calmer. I am at peace and at rest. My thoughts, which lead to my actions, become more purposeful and effective, especially when we are in God's plan, performing His will.

"Whatever is commendable [admirable]." What do I admire? Do I envy what I admire? Finding things or people to admire is a good thing, especially if they are Godly. If I admire something true, noble, right, pure, lovely, and good, it should inspire me to do likewise.

The Bible doesn't really address the idea of what is admirable; however, there is one brief reference that reminds us of an example of what or who to admire. 2 Samuel 1:23 states, *"Saul and Jonathan — in life they were loved and admired, and in death they were not parted."* Frankly, I wouldn't agree with the reference to Saul, but I would agree with Jonathan, especially regarding his deep friendship with David, who became Saul's adversary or rival; that's a different story. Jonathan is someone we should admire. Jonathan, after all, was the supposed "crown prince" of Israel, yet he understood that David would instead follow and ascend to that throne, not him.

Who we really should admire is Jesus. Jesus is our ultimate model of whom to admire. Jesus' pedestal of admiration should be far higher than that of any other admirable people. Jesus' actions and teachings should be more admirable than anyone else's. This familiar passage from Hebrews may say it best:

Therefore, since we are surrounded by such a great cloud of witnesses, let us throw off everything that hinders and the sin that so easily entangles. And let us run with perseverance the race marked out for us, [2] fixing our eyes on Jesus, the pioneer and perfecter of faith. For the joy set before Him He endured the cross, scorning its shame, and sat down at the right hand of the throne of God. Hebrews 12:1-2.

"If anything is excellent or praiseworthy." Who or what, more than Jesus and His life, fulfills these two requirements? Excellence is a superlative. When something or someone is excellent, it is at its zenith; it can't get any better. Psalm 45:1-2 says,

My heart is stirred by a noble theme as I recite my verses for the king;
my tongue is the pen of a skillful writer.

[2] *You are the most excellent of men and your lips have been anointed with grace,*
since God has blessed you forever.

Although speaking of David, Jesus is the ultimate king who will forever sit on the Throne.

Praiseworthy? No other person, no other name is worthy of praise except for Jesus. The Bible tells us - and we've already discussed this - [10] *so that at the name of Jesus every knee should bow, in heaven and on earth and under the earth,* [11] *and every tongue confess that Jesus Christ is Lord, to the glory of God the Father.* Philippians 2:10-11.

The bottom line.

Paul practiced what he preached. He renewed his mind, making God, in all Three Persons, the focus of his attention. This attention was such that, regardless of his circumstances (the next lesson), he could not only find peace but indeed experience God's peace. The kind of peace that transcends all of our limited human understanding. Using Paul as a model (divine mentor) not only for ministry but also for daily living isn't a bad choice.

Even though Paul said to imitate him (as found in 1 Corinthians 4:19 and 2 Thessalonians 3:9), he was actually directing us, believers, to a higher standard. Paul was directing us to follow and imitate Jesus. Jesus is to be our focus for living.

In fact, Jesus encompasses all that we are to think about. Jesus is "faithful and true". He is the most noble man to have walked the earth. Jesus is "our righteousness"; without Him, we are sinful and lost. Jesus is pure; Jesus was the only man who lived a perfect and sinless life to then be crucified and die as an atonement for your sin and my sin in our place so that we might live eternally with Him in glory.

Jesus is lovely. He was - and still is - attractive in all ways. People wanted to be with Him, just for who He is and was. Jesus is admirable and praiseworthy. Jesus is Lord to the glory of God the Father. It is on Him that we should think. Jesus should consume our thoughts as we go through the day, as we meet our struggles and encounter those who are hurting and in need. Jesus should be the first person that comes to our mind when we are looking for someone to emulate.

It's all about Him; it's not about me.

Heavenly Father, thank You for setting before us a list that is more than just a checklist for the day. The life that You present before us each day is Your power to live an abundant, exciting, and rich life. As we read and study Your Word, will You please cleanse our hearts and minds for the purpose of polishing our life mirrors to better reflect You in all that we think, say, and do. May You receive the glory and honor, not us. Amen.

Finding Joy: Philippians, Regular Maintenance

Verses: Philippians 4:8-9; Galatians 5:22-25; Romans 1:18-32

Key Questions:

What needs maintenance in your life?

How do we transform our minds?

How do we produce Spiritual fruit?

The Noetic Effects of Sin:

The Solution to Transforming our minds:

1.

2.

3.

4.

5.

6.

7.

8.

The bottom line…

Homework: Think about how we can change or modify our thoughts and thought processes to become more like Jesus and find true Joy in this earthly life.

Finding Joy: Strong Enough

Sometimes we look at people who have or are going through a time of seemingly great difficulty and are amazed at their strength.

Those folks rarely ask for help (at least directly). To a certain degree, they may seem melancholy or "accepting" their circumstances. They seem neither mad nor disappointed, nor at the other end of the emotional spectrum, particularly happy or rejoicing. But you know that they are "content". They are "solid" in who they are.

When I originally wrote this lesson, I was, and still am, speaking from personal experience. For a number of years, almost a decade, my life was far from a bed of roses or complete ease. And yet, as Paul says throughout his letter to the Philippians, "I rejoice..." I echo his sentiment. I rejoiced then, and I continue to rejoice in what God continues to do in and through my life.

Coming to the end of this epistle and the end of this series, we're going to rejoice. Not as the world rejoices, but we will rejoice in holiness and awe at a God who loves us, cares for us, and in His mercy, has saved us for something exceedingly better.

Here's this last section of Philippians, chapter 4:

10 I rejoiced in the Lord greatly that now at length you have revived your concern for me. You
were indeed concerned for me, but you had no opportunity. 11 Not that I am speaking of
being in need, for I have learned, in whatever situation I am, to be content. 12 I know how to
be brought low, and I know how to abound. In any and every circumstance, I have learned
the secret of facing plenty and hunger, abundance and need. 13 I can do all things through
Him who strengthens me.

14 Yet it was kind of you to share my trouble. 15 And you Philippians yourselves know that in
the beginning of the gospel, when I left Macedonia, no church entered into partnership with
me in giving and receiving, except you only. 16 Even in Thessalonica you sent me help for my

needs once and again. [17] *Not that I seek the gift, but I seek the fruit that increases to your*
credit. [18] *I have received full payment, and more. I am well supplied, having received from*
Epaphroditus the gifts you sent, a fragrant offering, a sacrifice acceptable and pleasing to
God. [19] *And my God will supply every need of yours according to his riches in glory in Christ*
Jesus. [20] *To our God and Father be glory forever and ever. Amen.*

[21] *Greet every saint in Christ Jesus. The brothers who are with me greet you.* [22] *All the saints*
greet you, especially those of Caesar's household.

[23] *The grace of the Lord Jesus Christ be with your spirit.* Philippians 4:10-23.

God's Way of doing Life.

When you think about God, this Christian life that we live, and His economy, you have to realize that God does almost everything backwards, or at least from the opposite direction we would do it or expect it to be done. It's a strange dichotomy.

Weak is strong; empty is full; poor is rich; mournful is rejoicing. Those ideas don't seem to make any sense, do they? And yet they do, especially when examined from God's point of view.

Being a student of the great Jewish Rabbi Gamaliel, Paul had read the Scriptures. And now, as a minister of the Gospel of Christ, he would begin living the Scriptures. Paul would come to understand what God was speaking to His people. The following passage is a great example:

[28] *Do you not know?*
Have you not heard?
The Lord is the everlasting God,
the Creator of the ends of the earth.
He will not grow tired or weary,
and his understanding no one can fathom.

But let's look at these seven keys to understanding God's way of life and living as a believer.

One. It's not about my Ease.

We were designed to work. When God formed Adam and Eve, they had a job to do: tend the Garden that God provided. He didn't create us to sit around and enjoy a life of leisure. We are to rest when needed, but we are to be busy about the Father's work, and sometimes that involves certain hardships. Paul writes:

[7] or because of these surpassingly great revelations. Therefore, in order to keep me from
becoming conceited, I was given a thorn in my flesh, a messenger of Satan, to torment me.
[8] Three times I pleaded with the Lord to take it away from me. [9] But he said to me, "My grace
is sufficient for you, for my power is made perfect in weakness." Therefore I will boast all the
more gladly about my weaknesses, so that Christ's power may rest on me. [10] That is why, for
Christ's sake, I delight in weaknesses, in insults, in hardships, in persecutions, in difficulties.
For when I am weak, then I am strong. 2 Corinthians 12:7-10.

We will all face obstacles as we pursue God and His plan for our lives. Some will be mental. Some will be physical. Some will be financial or relational. The Bible is riddled with men and women who struggled and, more often than not, faced severe hardships doing God's work. And as they moved forward, God went before them, protecting them on all sides. That's what He promises to do for you and me as well.

Two. It's not about my Riches.

Our riches are spit. Like our "good works", they're like filthy rags. They are nothing in comparison to God's riches. The fact is, whatever we "have" was never really ours anyway. Whatever we have or possess was God's first. But His riches are abundant and glorious. We may live off the scraps of His table, but even those are a regular bounty.

[4] For this reason I kneel before the Father, [15] from whom every family in heaven and on earth
derives its name. [16] I pray that out of his glorious riches he may strengthen you with power

through his Spirit in your inner being, [17] *so that Christ may dwell in your hearts through faith. And I pray that you, being rooted and established in love,* [18] *may have power, together with all the Lord's holy people, to grasp how wide and long and high and deep is the love of Christ,* [19] *and to know this love that surpasses knowledge—that you may be filled to the measure of all the fullness of God.* Ephesians 3:14-19.

Even more, God's riches enrich every facet of our lives. As we see in this passage, His riches strengthen us and provide power, wisdom, faith, and love. Temporal or worldly riches cannot provide any of that.

God's wealth is the universe, but we argue over scraps. Ask God to provide and allow Him to open the floodgates of blessing on your life. You'll be amazed and then humbled by His love for you.

Three. It's not about my Victories.

Like my riches, my victories are nothing compared to His. God's victories are for His glory. God doesn't share His glory with us, but He does share His joy in the victories!

Paul reminds us:

[57] *But thanks be to God! He gives us the victory through our Lord Jesus Christ.*

[58] *Therefore, my dear brothers and sisters, stand firm. Let nothing move you. Always give yourselves fully to the work of the Lord, because you know that your labor in the Lord is not in vain.* 1 Corinthians 15:57-58.

We have already won the battle, beloved! If you are a Christian, you are already an heir to the Kingdom. Jesus's triumph over sin and death is the ultimate victory.

It is also the victory that forms the foundation of every other victory God will provide in our lives as we live for Him. How victorious! How good is our God!

Four. It's not my Salvation.

How is Paul able to "stand firm" himself? As I mentioned, Paul knew God and His Word. Scripture was captured in his heart and mind, and he could refer to it at will (assisted, of course, by the Holy Spirit). Aside from the Isaiah passage above, I suspect that Paul also hid in his heart the following:

2 *Surely God is my salvation;*
I will trust and not be afraid.
The Lord, the Lord himself, is my strength and my defense;
he has become my salvation."
3 *With joy you will draw water*
from the wells of salvation. Isaiah 12:2-3.

Or how about Job:

25 *I know that my redeemer lives,*
and that in the end he will stand on the earth.
26 *And after my skin has been destroyed,*
yet in my flesh I will see God;
27 *I myself will see him*
with my own eyes—I, and not another.
How my heart yearns within me! Job 19:25-27.

KNOWING that our salvation is God's free gift is an awesome thing. Without Christ, we can do nothing. Without Christ in our lives, we are nothing. It's all about Him and His finished work on the Cross—nothing more and nothing less.

Five. It's not about my Strength.

Like my riches, my strength is worthless compared to what God wants to do and can do in my life. What the Bible says is absolutely true: when I am weak, He is strong. And God is strong beyond my comprehension. He is always there for me, especially when my causes are His.

The Psalmist writes:

1 *I lift up my eyes to the mountains—*
where does my help come from?
2 *My help comes from the Lord,*
the Maker of heaven and earth.

3 *He will not let your foot slip—*
he who watches over you will not slumber;
4 *indeed, he who watches over Israel*
will neither slumber nor sleep.

5 *The Lord watches over you—*
the Lord is your shade at your right hand;
6 *the sun will not harm you by day,*
nor the moon by night.

7 *The Lord will keep you from all harm—*
he will watch over your life;
8 *the Lord will watch over your coming and going*
both now and forevermore. Psalm 121.

My help is not far off. I just have to look up, and He is there, waiting and willing not only to help, but also, many times, to carry me. God knows that He has asked us – each one of us - to do the impossible. And then in His grace, He will provide everything necessary to accomplish those impossible tasks, including the strength to carry me (us) through. With God, nothing is impossible. If I believe God created all that I can and can't see, then, He can absolutely tend for all my needs.

Six. It's not about my Plans.

Let's face it, our plans usually stink. We live and operate in the here and now. God's plans are so much better because he knows the end from the beginning and every last little bit in between.

Then there's this familiar reminder from the book of Jeremiah:

[11] *For I know the plans I have for you," declares the Lord, "plans to prosper you and not to harm you, plans to give you hope and a future.* [12] *Then you will call on me and come and pray to me, and I will listen to you.* [13] *You will seek me and find me when you seek me with all your heart.* Jeremiah 29:11-13.

Paul could not only cling to these passages of God's Word but also read the biographies of God's beloved saints. These servants of God would become Paul's Divine Mentors. They would teach Paul so that Paul could teach the Philippians then and us today.

In the end, Paul was a great encourager, and he was sufficiently strong because of two things: First, he made himself subject to God, the Sovereign of the Universe, and the lover of his own soul. Second, Paul was other-centered - he served others by preaching the Gospel first. He had his priorities very straight. Paul was willing to accept discipline for himself and to pass it along when required. God was first, other people were second, and his own life and needs were somewhere after that.

And that was okay with the apostle.

And that should be okay with you and me, which leads us to the final key.

Seven. It's not about my Life.

Knowing that we are living for Him first, others next, and me last is a paradigm shift in our thinking. Knowing that ultimately makes the mission that He has given us easier. Yes, we can do all things through Christ who strengthens us. How do we know that? Paul tells us in verse 19:

[19] And my God will supply every need of yours according to his riches in glory in Christ Jesus.

Paul says that God "WILL" meet our needs. There's no doubt about that. He's not fudging or hesitating. He knows, and so should we, that God WILL provide for us. We are not to question how or when, because He WILL!

And we can know that because God is rich beyond our wildest dreams. We have a guarantee of the riches of Christ. What are the riches of Christ, you ask? I may not be a theologian, but I would give you a one-word answer (maybe a word and a phrase): the Universe and everything in it.

How's that for riches? Paul wants all of his students - you and me - to understand that fact and be encouraged to stand firm and press on. Because we are heirs to the Kingdom, we can claim these riches. We don't claim them for ourselves or for our direct benefit, but we claim them so that we may glorify God. And that's usually where we get tripped up: we want the glory (it can be subtle or blatant) rather than making sure God is the recipient.

Ours is not to be anxious for anything. Ours is not to be tossed about like a wave or a reed in the wind. Paul was *"amply supplied"* - and so are we. We are to be content and secure in all things solely because of the promises of God and the riches of God. They are all His to give away to us, His beloved. God is pleased to supply His children at His whim, will, and direction.

We are to be content in whatever circumstance God has placed us. When we know that His plans and purposes are right for our lives, we shouldn't be anxious. Our contentment not only acknowledges God's provision but also His loving care for His children. He provides the strength we need and the provisions to stand firm. Your job and my job are merely to obey and love. To obey God's will in and for our lives is better oftentimes than praise and worship (especially when we then don't obey). When we obey, we love God. When we obey, we should love others in the spheres of influence God has placed us in.

That's what Paul did. More importantly, that's what Jesus did and does. They obeyed to glorify the Father. We are strong enough because of His loving provision.

Let's end in a moment of prayer...

My God and Father, I pray to you. So many of us struggle and are struggling in these times. The world is in utter turmoil. Our lives and relationships are fractured if not broken. We are often scared of what is happening around us. We need help with our finances. We are unworthy of your love, yet You give it freely. Help us to accept all that You want and are willing to give as we live our lives as a testament to Your love and Grace. Supply us abundantly. Help us to be content in all circumstances. Help us to love others first. May you receive the honor and the glory always. Amen.

Finding Joy: Philippians, Strong Enough

Verses: Philippians 4:10-20, Isaiah 40:28-31, Ephesian 3:14-19, 1 Corinthians 15:57-58

Key Questions:
What is God's way of doing things?
What does it mean to be "strong" and "satisfied"?

God's way of doing Life:

Isaiah 40:28-31

How are we satisfied? What things or people cause you to be or feel satisfied in life?

Being a student of life means that we must become a student of God:

1. Not my ease

2. Not my riches

3. Not my victories

4. Not my salvation

5. Not my strength

6. Not my plans

7. Not my life

Homework: Look back at your life. Look at where you were in those hard times and contrast that to where God has brought you to today. Regularly making the time to reflect back is good as it provides the proper perspective we all need.

Weeping may tarry for the night, but joy comes with the morning. Psalm 30:5

Finding Joy: Therefore...

If you thought Philippians was all about "joy", then what's the "therefore" there for?

People refer to Paul's epistle to the Philippians as the "book of joy" because the word "joy" and its derivatives (joy, rejoice) are used about 16 times throughout the letter. And then there is the word "therefore". As Dr. Howard Hendricks puts it (paraphrasing), "whenever you see the word 'therefore', you should ask yourself what it's there for." Paul regularly uses the word "therefore" in his writings. By my count, he uses it 72 times (not including the epistle to the Hebrews - another 16 times - if Paul indeed wrote it), throughout his writings.

And the word "therefore" is there for a purpose: to cause the reader (you and me) to stop and pay attention because Paul is about to bring a truth to the forefront based on what he has already written.

As we come to the end and wrap up this study through the Book of Philippians, let's recap by going back and noting those "therefores" and what comes before and after them. This study is presented on the premise that Philippians is a series of life lessons that everyone encounters and struggles with, especially the Christian. The good news is that Paul reminds us we can live "better" as Christians. We don't necessarily have life any easier or simpler (take Paul's life, for example). Still, we can go through these situations more completely because of our personal relationship with God through Jesus Christ.

There are five "therefores" in Philippians and two "yets" (another conjunct that's used to join phrases, sentences, or ideas).

"Yet which shall I choose?" Philippians 1:22. Good question! All of us struggle with this question. Paul acknowledges that life is oftentimes difficult. He would rather be in Heaven enjoying His divine reward, but he wrestles with God's call on his life to bring and preach the Gospel to the Gentile world.

the Godhead, Father, Son, and Holy Spirit, work in absolute unity and harmony to forward their purposes and plans.

The life lesson here is this: if you are in active ministry - regardless of its simplicity or complexity - you can't (and better not) do it alone. All you need are a couple of good, loving, hardworking friends to help take away some of the burden (especially the mundane aspects). And by the way, as a reminder to all of us: Life itself is a ministry!

Therefore, my brothers, whom I love and long for, *my joy and crown, stand firm thus in the Lord, my beloved.* Philippians 4:1.

This "therefore" actually looks back at everything Paul said in chapter three. Paul almost reiterates the struggles of life, including who we are, who we believe we are, and who others (especially non-believers) believe we are. Our heavenly credentials should be all that matters.

Using those credentials, we are better able to "press on" towards God's goals for His Kingdom and our lives. This life is a marathon. We have to pace ourselves according to God's Word and Will. If we don't, we can and sometimes will burn out trying. Furthermore, we don't want to look at our credentials outside God's context or His rules. We are to always (as much as humanly possible) be in His Word, reading and studying the Scriptures.

Why should we be doing this? Not for our own knowledge and pride to show off, but to better know God and Who He is and what His Plans and goals are. Putting ourselves in the right perspective eliminates a lot of stress.

That's our life lesson: saturate yourself with God's Word to better know Him, to better relate with the people and situations He has placed in our lives, and to "therefore" live the abundant life He has promised.

"Yet it was kind of you to share my troubles." Philippians 4:14.

This almost sounds like a melancholy-ish statement, but it's not. Paul is not resigned to his situation (imprisonment). Still, he is content with his circumstances, and he wants his Philippian children to understand that there is much more to life than a nice home and fancy transportation (yes, they struggled with those issues two thousand years ago, too).

I don't know about you, but whether I like it or not, I've learned a lot more about life and living through adversity. Tough or trying times demonstrate to me not only that God is in control, but also that He really and truly loves me. He won't necessarily prevent me from participating in a tough, or even life-changing, situation, but He won't abandon me either; God will always see me through it. And when I've gone through it (whatever it is), I can look back and marvel at what God has accomplished, which is even more amazing.

With that Truth, all of us can agree with Paul when he wrote: *19 And my God will supply every need of yours according to his riches in glory in Christ Jesus.* verse 19.

A couple of conclusions.

With these "therefores," we can draw a couple of conclusions about how this little letter to the Philippian church is full of foundational life lessons.

The first conclusion is that Christianity is completely relevant to our lives and to every single person's life around us. So often we hear (erroneously) that the Bible is not "relevant" to life in American or Western twenty-first-century society and culture. The fact of the matter is that man hasn't really changed in two thousand years. We continue to struggle with poverty and substance abuse. There continues to be much strife and envy across cultures and peoples. The only difference is that we've become much more sophisticated (or so we believe) in our thinking and actions (and technology).

The Christian believer who reads their Bible each day and prays for their family, friends, and co-workers, while wrestling with the hurts of this world, is a gift to the unsaved and unbelieving world that there is hope and more to life than simply chasing after stuff and experiences.

We have a relevant story to tell and answers to provide. Granted, they may not always be what people want to hear, but very often God's Truth is hard and sharp. We are, after all, living and playing according to God's specific rules. And you know what? His rules are completely just, 100% fair and equal, regardless of time or circumstance, no matter how difficult or hurtful they may be.

God wants us to be transformed into the image of Christ. We are created in the image of God, but we have been corrupted by sin, which is our nature. Sin has corrupted every one of us and so disfigured us as it were. And so God lovingly and purposefully remolds and reshapes us into how we should be.

The second conclusion we draw from these life lessons is that there is no life worth living without God. As I have struggled with the many issues of family, business, and relationships over the past several years, I cannot begin to understand how I could survive apart from God. As my friend Charlie reminds me, I have to continually "lean in" to God. I have to depend on Him for everything, every day, completely. As I watch my unbelieving friends deal with similar issues and have nowhere to turn to except stuff and habits that are actually detrimental to their well-being, I often shake my head and wonder, how can you not accept God's gift of salvation through Jesus?

And so, I have to be an imitator of Christ - daily - and praise Him for what He has done, what He is doing, and what He will do in my life and circumstances.

Paul makes it very clear in Philippians that Jesus is Who He says He is: God incarnate. Jesus came to save us from our sins and to be reconciled to God for eternal life, rather than being punished and condemned to eternal death. And all of that is contingent upon Jesus's atoning and self-sacrificial death on the Cross two thousand years ago. There is nothing else that can reconcile us to God; it is the Cross alone.

Furthermore, we must not forget that we come to the Cross as individuals. Not as a group. Not as a family - although we do become a family.

Others may show us the way, or pray us there, but in all reality, we come alone, drawn only by the power of the Holy Spirit working in our lives.

That's it. That is the Gospel that Paul lived to speak and demonstrate, so that the Philippian church and all who would follow in the years, decades, and centuries to come would live abundantly now in this temporal life as a preparation for an incredible life in eternity with our Lord and Savior, Jesus Christ.

Therefore, let us now go forward reflecting His light and love to a lost and dying world seeking answers.

May we pray…

Loving Father and Wonderful Savior, thank you for this letter to the Philippian church and the life lessons that Paul strove to put forward. Your words, penned by this man, show us how to live life abundantly, although we may struggle from time to time. We thank you that your yoke is easy compared to what the world wants to give us. You bid us to come to you as we are and take your free gift of salvation and everlasting life. Thank you for loving us even though we don't deserve it. Help us to reflect Jesus in all that we think, say, and do. Be with us always, we pray. Amen.

Finding Joy: Philippians, Therefore

Verses: Philippians

Key Question:

What is the "therefore" there for?

How does the Christian do life "better" than the non-Christian?

"Yets" & "Therefores":

Yet:

Therefore:

Therefore:

Therefore:

Therefore:

Therefore:

Yet:

Two Conclusions:

1.

2.

Homework (for the rest of your life): Understand that at many times and circumstances that life is hard. Find Joy! Look for beauty. Look for kindness. Look for the peace that only God can provide. When you find those things, you will find Joy. That's God's promise!

Final Thoughts of Joy

As I finish up some final editing before publishing this study, the Holy Spirit has brought to mind a time in my life that needs to be mentioned.

In my former career as a small-business owner in the swimming pool and hot tub industry, God brought many different people into my business to serve them well. One such person was Jeremiah McKenzie.

Before I recount this divine appointment, but without going into great detail, the time was the mid-2000s (2005 to 2008). There were tremendous business pressures as we took on significant debt through a hefty mortgage. Our family was struggling with finding the correct resources to help us and the needs of our older son; there was terrible stress on the five of us. In my quest for "normalcy" in daily life, I made the mistake of plunging myself into my business, telling my wife I needed to work harder and longer to support our current and future financial needs, while now neglecting my wife's and children's needs as a husband and father. I even bought into the deception that by attending Bible study with my friends on Saturday mornings and church on Sundays, well then, my acting "holy" would make everything "swell" or "fine".

It didn't, and it wasn't.

And then Jeremiah McKenzie came into my store one day. Before going on, I'll tell you that this episode didn't necessarily "solve" anything, but God used it as a time of instruction.

Jeremiah had absolutely nothing to offer me. He was the overseeing bishop of a small congregation of Jamaican Americans. He lived with his daughter in a small apartment. He was a very humble man in his late seventies, with few extravagant possessions, except one: the entire Bible he had hidden in his heart and mind. He was able to bring any Scripture passage to mind and quote it in proper context for the exact need of that moment. Through the lenses of his old, thick glasses shone eyes of love for all, devotion to his calling, and a captivating, peaceful walk with God.

So, on this one weekday morning, Bishop McKenzie walked into my store. He told my salesperson that he wanted to speak to the owner. I came down to greet him, and he asked me my name, asked me if I was a Christian, then proclaimed, "Brother Ron, (he always called me brother Ron) I was driving by, and God told me to stop here because YOU would be able to take care of a need that I have for my church. People need to be baptized, and we need a proper baptismal pool. How soon can you make this all happen?" Yes, Bishop McKenzie was always direct and to the point.

In my twenty-plus years as a Christian, I had never personally met such a man before. Jeremiah was a man who had nothing, yet, because of his relationship with Jesus, he knew he had everything he needed to live and minister in this world. I saw that he had something that I sorely lacked, and that was Joy – God's joy; and with that joy, there was peace. In short order, we became close friends, and just that simple relationship was exactly what I needed to traverse our business and family struggles at that time.

What I remember most about Jeremiah was that I could come to him and pour out my heart with all its burdens. He listened and then told me to get back to "praising and working." He would tell me, "Brother Ron, praise the Lord! When you walk into your store or into church or into your home, and you know there's a struggle, lift up your hands and PRAISE HIM! Praise the Lord with SHOUTS of Joy! God knows exactly what you need and when you'll need it, so just praise Him!"

I can still hear his voice with that easy-going, yet firm, Jamaican accent today.

God, in His loving kindness, has provided for all our needs in so many "common" ways. God loves us so much that He even provides us with the beauty of flowers, chirping birds, and awesome sunrises and sunsets in the midst of our struggles. He provides us with the experience of hearing the laughter of little children, or the sweet touch of an elderly saint who wants to sit for a cup of tea, or maybe a simple text message from a friend we haven't seen or spoken to for a while, asking how we're doing. For us dog lovers, He gives us the nuzzle of a companion who loves us for who we are, regardless of how good or bad our day was.

I am thankful beyond measure for my friendship with Jeremiah McKenzie, who has been called Home by his Lord and Savior. I'm sure that Jeremiah heard the words that we all long to hear, *"Well done, good and faithful servant! Enter into the joy of your Master!"* Matthew 25:23

A simple man, leading a simple life of devotion to his God and Creator. A simple man whom God used to make a big difference in my life of turmoil and to help me find true Joy.

And now, several verses to remind us of finding joy as we wrap up our study and keep a proper perspective on "hard times". The first one is from Jesus's half-brother James. James writes, *"2 Count it all joy, my brothers, when you meet trials of various kinds, 3 for you know that the testing of your faith produces steadfastness. 4 And let steadfastness have its full effect, that you may be perfect and complete, lacking in nothing."* James 1:2-4

And then there's the apostle Paul, whose letter to the Philippians we've been studying. Without doubt, Paul knew and understood hard times. More importantly, Paul understood that with Jesus, he would get through those hard times, because they were there for a divine reason. A couple of Paul's closing statements in chapter four: *"I rejoiced..." "I know how to be brought low..." "I have learned the secret of facing hunger and need..."* How can Paul know and do all this? Because of his personal relationship with Jesus, Paul could say, *"I can do all things through Him who strengthens me"* and *"my God will supply every need according to His riches in glory in Christ Jesus."*

Paul leaned entirely into his God and Savior, all the time. We can too.

THAT is a God who loves His children and wants the best for them. That is a heavenly Father who knows and can provide for our every need.

Through it all, I choose to find Joy. It is my prayer for you that you would and will find joy, regardless of the situations or circumstances, because God has already provided it. May you also find His Joy.

Our God is always good. Always!

Appendix – Study Leader's Notes

If you're leading this study in Sunday School or a small group, use the session notes on the next pages. These are my personal notes, updated after leading different various groups.

As a leader or facilitator, our task is to complete the "homework" and chapter notes as we study the Scriptures to prepare for leading our group. Leaders should spend time reading God's Word, consulting references, and praying before meeting the group. God expects more from us in time, commitment, and grace as we disciple and support others.

Bible verses may be referenced but not quoted. Review them beforehand so you and your group understand the related concepts. Key Verses and Key Questions are your starting points. Always begin and end with Scripture.

During your lesson preparation, it is worthwhile to compare various translations for discussion and clarification/clarity.

When you see a Key Verse, read it and the surrounding passage for context—especially if a single verse is noted. Always provide the proper context to help everyone understand the meaning.

The leaders' notes are in larger and bolder print to assist when standing at a lectern in front of a group.

Guide your group's thoughts, discussions, and prayers. Remember, God's Word and the Holy Spirit are the true teachers.

Many around the world are praying for you and your group. Let's begin and trust God's leading as we seek renewed power in prayer!

Finding Joy: Philippians, Pray First

Verses: Acts 16:6-40, Philippians 1:1-11

Key Questions:
What's so special about Philippi?
Why do we need to pray for others?

Why Philippi:

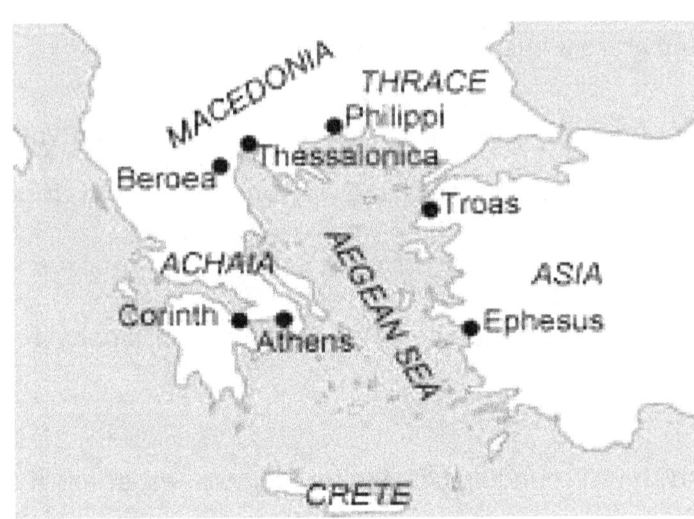

gateway to Macedonia from Asia Minor

Via Egnatia

gentiles only, no synagogue, un-churched polytheists

a lot like us today...

Purposely Praying for People: we pray in order to...

Encourage

"I thank my God [for] you...", "I always pray with joy...", "I have you in my heart...", "I long for all of you with affection..."

Encouragement to press on, keep going

How do you feel personally when you read Philippians 1:3-11?

How are you personally encouraged by reading those verses?

Instruct or Teach – Christian living, doctrine,

the *"prayer of a righteous man is powerful and effective"*, James 5:16, what are we really saying?

Instructing others to seek out God's will & plan rather than our will

Confidence – v 6

Grace – v 7

Discernment – v 9-10

What do we learn from verses 6 – 10

Remind

The affection of Jesus is a 2-way street

A reminder that the unbelieving world is always watching us

In a plastic world, people are looking for "real"

How do our non-Christian friends look at today's world? How do we best or better answer them?

Remind ourselves that we are all works in progress, God will complete His work in & through our lives

Remind ourselves to give glory to God

Homework: Think about how you're praying for others. Continue praying for others by name.

Finding Joy: Philippians, Homesick

Verses: Philippians 1:12 – 30

Key Questions:
What is the importance of "Christ being preached"?

How are we to be "heavenly minded" and "earthly good"?

Paul in chains & in conflict:

v. 12-18

What was going on in the Imperial palace?

How did Paul feel about other preachers of Christ?

v. 19-30

Why was Paul conflicted?

Was Jesus conflicted?

Compare their lives as <u>men</u>

So, since we're all stranded here:

Conduct ourselves in a Godly fashion

Are we showing or is Jesus being reflected?

Stand firm in the Spirit

How do we stand firm?

Strive together in the Gospel

Do we understand how to succinctly pronounce the Gospel?

Saved by God

Why can't we save ourselves?

Homework: How are you striving to present the Gospel to those in your sphere of influence?

Finding Joy: Philippians, Attitude Adjustment

Verses: Philippians 2:1 – 11, 1 Corinthians 13:1 – 13, 2 Corinthians 6:3 – 9, 2 Corinthians 5:16 – 20

Key Questions:

What does it mean "*Your attitude should be the same as that of Christ Jesus*"_ ?

How are we to act having that attitude?

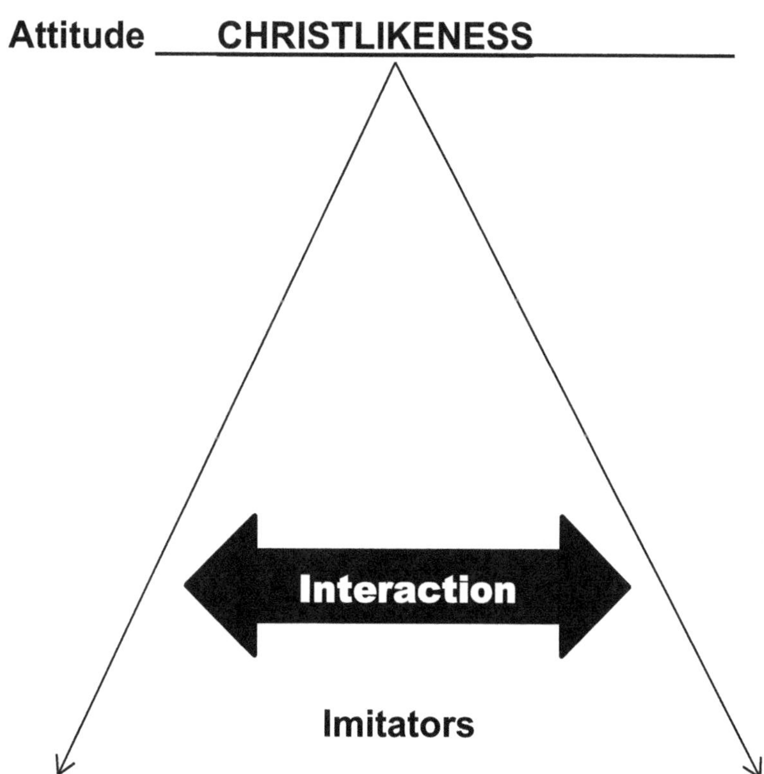

Action IMITATORS **Action RECONCILORS**

Homework: The Gospel is a mirror for our daily living. With every action & interaction, are we leading a successful & fruitful life because of a good attitude?

Finding Joy: Philippians, Jesus Christ, His Deity and Humanity

SPECIAL NOTE: THIS LESSON MAY NEED TO BE BROKEN INTO TWO DISCUSSIONS AS THERE IS MUCH TO REVIEW. DON'T RUSH THROUGH IT!

Key Questions:

Why Jesus?

Why is Jesus being fully God and fully Man important?

What do we do with Jesus?

Hypostasis or Hypostatic Union - The essential person of Jesus in which his human and divine natures are united.

Homo-ousian – same essence or nature (the Father & the Son)

Expiation vs. Propitiation

Expiation – atoning, atonement; covers or removes sin. Examples of human expiation.

Propitiation – expiation PLUS having the idea of Sacrificing ALL of God's demands. If Jesus were just a "godly" man, so what? Man is not sinless; he is not 100% just, holy, righteous, etc. Then really anyone could have died for our sins. If Jesus is truly God, then God taking on all of our sins & putting them away - expiating them - will only satisfy God & therefore the full Propitiation.

Philippians 2:6-11, Hebrews. 1:1-4

What are the historical, philosophical, and religious struggles that we have today regarding Jesus?

How did the waters get so muddy?

Schools of thought – Antiochene & Alexandrian

Antiochene – could be either man or God at one time, not both

Alexandrian – not completely human, divine nature more important

Council of Nicea (325 AD) - purpose of the council was to resolve disagreements arising from within the Church of Alexandria over the nature of Jesus in relationship to the Father; in particular, whether Jesus was the literal son of God or was he a figurative son, like the other "sons of God" in the Bible. – Arian heresy – Result: Nicene Creed & Athanasius (secretary to Bishop Alexander)

Council of Chalcedon (451 AD) – Christ was IN 2 natures, not OF 2 natures

The Confession of Chalcedon:

“Following the holy Fathers, we unanimously teach and confess one and the same Son, our Lord Jesus Christ: the same perfect in divinity and perfect in humanity, the same truly God and truly man, composed of rational soul and body; consubstantial with the Father as to his divinity and consubstantial with us as to his humanity; "like us in all things but sin." He was begotten from the Father before all ages as to his divinity and in these last days, for us and for our salvation, was born as to his humanity of the virgin Mary, the Mother of God.

We confess that one and the same Christ, Lord, and only-begotten Son, is to be acknowledged in two natures without confusion, change, division, or separation (in duabus naturis inconfuse, immutabiliter, indivise, inseparabiliter). The distinction between natures was never abolished by their union, but rather the character proper to each of the two natures was preserved as they came together in one person (prosopon) and one hypostasis."

Doctrine of the Kenosis – what did God the Son do to become Jesus the Christ?

Kenosis – Definition: to relinquish, set-aside, divest of attributes. "made himself of no reputation"

The Problem of the "God-Man" – the mathematics of the problem

Addition – did God add on the "limitations" of humanity

Subtraction – did God, as Jesus, subtract part of His deity

Choice – choosing NOT to use versus giving up. Nonuse does not equal subtraction

Proofs of Jesus' Humanity – provide Biblical passages or verses that support these ideas

Human body – born, developed as a human, lived, died

Human soul & spirit – men & women have souls & spirits, animals don't

Human characteristics – hunger, exhaustion, thirst, emotions (love, compassion, anger), experienced temptation

Possessed human names – Jesus, Son of Man,

Proofs of Jesus' deity – provide Biblical passages or verses that support these ideas

In His Incarnation –

Angels announced His coming

Conceived by the Holy Spirit

Virgin birth

Fulfilled prophesy

angelic worship

accepted human worship

taught in the temple

In His Ministry –

Fulfilled prophesy

Father confirmed Him with the Holy Spirit

revealed His glory – mount of Transfiguration

dealt directly with Satan

healed people

raised the dead

forgave sin

accepted worship (& had the right to accept)

lived a completely sinless life

In His Death & Resurrection –

Fulfilled prophesy

forgave sin

healed people

raised the dead – especially Himself

dealt directly with Satan – took the keys of death away

accepted worship

willingly gave up His life

took on a new Body

ascended into Heaven

sat down at the right hand of God

Final discussion:

So, what do we do with Jesus?

We either accept Him and His atoning life, death, and resurrection as a one-time payment for our sins, which is God's gift of grace, spending eternity with Him, or we reject Jesus and suffer the penalty for our sins, which is eternal separation from God. God sent Jesus in His love for us. He will not force us in either direction since Love is a choice.

After examining all there is about the birth, life, death, and resurrection of Jesus, of what importance is He to your life?

John 11:45 – 52

Finding Joy: Philippians, Shine

Verses: Philippians 2:12 – 18, Matthew 5:16; 13:37-43

Key Questions:

What does it mean to "work out your salvation with fear & trembling"?

What is the purpose of the Christian being "shiny"?

Is it works or faith?:

How do we bring "light" into the world?

Who brings in the light? Matthew 6:22-23

What is light tied to? Matthew 5:16, 13:37-43

Purposes of "light" in our lives:

1. Transparency – light shows us our own sin & shortcomings – the working out part

2. Expose the Darkness – Christians are not only salt (a preservative) but LIGHT. Light purifies.

3. Points to the Cross – everything is rubbish without the Cross.

What is the Gospel? Page 55

What distinguishes "light" from "darkness"?

"Light" can equal:

Homework: You are in control of your own dimmer switch. Are you turning it up or down?

Finding Joy: Philippians, a Few Good Friends

Verses: Philippians 2:19 – 30; Ecclesiastes 4:9; 1 Thessalonians 5:11

Key Questions:

Why do we need friends in ministry?

Who is a friend in the ministry God gave you?

Who is Timothy:

Acts 16:1-3

Why is Timothy's ministry important?

Who is Epaphroditus:

Apparently, a citizen of Philippi, later first bishop of Philippi. Not to be confused with Epaphras from Colossi

Name & reflect on two Friends (not including your spouse) in your ministry:

1.

2.

Homework: Publicly acknowledge a friend or co-worker in the ministry that God has given you.

Finding Joy: Philippians, the Right Credentials

Verses: Philippians 3:1 - 11

Key Questions:

What are your credentials for Ministry?

What is “rubbish”?

Of the world:

In the world:

How are these 2 ideas contrasted?

Through the verses:

The Centrality of the Cross…

What were Paul’s credentials?

What is truly important when it comes to Credentials?

Two takeaways:

1. **What about your credentials?**

   earthly or heavenly?

2. **It's all about the Cross**

Homework: Think about how the credentials God has given you should be presented.

Finding Joy: Philippians, Pressing On

Verses: Philippians 3:12 – 4:1; 1 Corinthians 9:24-25; 2 Timothy 4:7-8

Key Questions:

What is your goal or focus?

Do you know & understand your purpose in God's Plan?

Of racing & mountain tops…

What is Paul's fascination with racing?

1 & 2 Corinthians, Galatians, Ephesians (as quoted in Acts 20) and 2 Timothy

Through the verses:

Four Points:

1. **Understanding who & Whose we are**… defining our Divine Credentials

   Jesus took hold us first, not the other way around … idea of election

God's race, using His rules.

Participants as well as spectators

Where were you on life's journey when God got a hold of YOU?

2. Accepting that fact…

2 Corinthians 5:16-18
We're not "like" something new; we ARE new! Accept that fact.

our individual thoughts & attitudes about God speak volumes

A. W. Tozer wrote in his book "The Knowledge of the Holy": *"What comes to your mind when you think about God is the most important thing about you...".*

stop living in the past. Put it behind you. Focus on God's goal for your life.

3. Understanding the nature of those around us – the contrast of believer v. unbeliever…

World is corrupt & dying. World is running a different race.

hamster wheel analogy

"Do you not know that in a race all the runners run, but only one gets the prize? Run in such a way as to get the prize. Everyone who competes in the games goes into strict training. They do it to get a crown that will not last; but we do it to get a crown that will last forever." 1 Corinthians 9:24-25.

vs. unbeliever who is an enemy & passage following… 18 – 21

world is not "eagerly" awaiting a Savior, especially in the guise of Jesus…

4. **Our relationship with fellow believers**…

Running but also standing firm…

Galatians 5:7 says and asks: *"You were running a good race. Who cut in on you and kept you from obeying the truth?"*

We must run with blinders & help our brothers & sisters with adjusting their blinders

"I have fought the good fight, I have finished the race, I have kept the faith. Now there is in store for me the crown of righteousness, which the Lord, the righteous Judge, will award

to me on that day — and not only to me, but also to all who have longed for his appearing." 2 Timothy 4:7-8

Homework: What blinders do you need to successfully run your race?

Finding Joy: Philippians, Anxiety, Depression & Restoration

IMPORTANT: These are the notes for both sessions. The group leader should use their judgment to determine the pace of the discussion. A recommendation would be to discuss the problem the first week and the solution the following session.

Verses: Philippians 4:2-9, 1 Corinthians 10:13,

Questions to answer:

What can bring about anxiety & disrupted relationships?

How do we bring restoration?

The Problem:

Euodia & Syntyche are having issues that have the potential of disrupting the Philippian church in general.

Sometimes working together – family, profession or ministry – can lead to tensions. Unresolved tensions will lead to further personal as well as interpersonal problems

Just because a family, business or organization – even a church – is good-looking on the outside, doesn't mean that it is healthy

Sometimes it takes more than simply "clearing the air"

The Downward Cycle of Anxiety & Depression:

S – Strife or the Situation.

Until you recognize & understand the situation, you can't deal with it.

Sin is a part of all of our lives. It is part of our nature.

Notice the "markers" along the way throughout the epistle: Philippians 1:27; 2:3-4, 12-14; 3:13

A – Anxiety.

Living in Anxiety – whatever the cause - may cause us to be consumed by it. We keep playing with the anxiety rather than dealing with it.

Are we living in GIGO (Garbage In – Garbage Out)?

Matthew 6:25-27

D - Depression

Call it what it is & get help. Don't let your pride get in the way.

You need perspective.

Depression hurts mentally, physically, emotionally & interpersonally.

D – Disagreement with others

When we are in our own depression, we will look for the faults in others to make ourselves "feel" better → leads to arguments

We must look for some type of common ground

Think about – possibly discuss – past disagreements. How were they worked out?

D – Disruption in Human Relationship

What's so lovely about a church full of disrupted humans? No wonder the world sees us as hypocrites and no better than themselves.

D – Disruption in our Relationship with God

How can you say that you have a "good" relationship with God if your relationship with your wife or child or whomever is disrupted?

Prayer time, reading time, personal worship time is disrupted

Matthew 5:23-24

R – Restoration

The path to restoration starts with recognizing Who God is as well as who we are.

Psalm 34:17-20

The Solution:

1 Corinthians 10:13 & the steps found in Colossians

The Upward Climb toward Restoration:

R – Restore our Relationship with God

Begin getting the garbage & clutter out of our lives & put God first

Matthew 12:34 is so true; we speak what is in our hearts

Philippians 4:8-9

O – bring Order to our lives

Clean the inside of the cup: Matthew 23:25

Colossians 2:5, 2:7, 3:8-9, 3:12-17

R – Restore our interpersonal relationships

God first, then move on to the people in our lives

Sometimes we have to deal with “poopy diapers”. God calls us to Grace

A – disagreements become Agreements

This may be a gradual process where each side has to systematically lay aside personal pride & surrender, finding mutual agreement, majoring on the majors; agreeing to disagree on the minors

A – anxiety becomes Acceptance

Acceptance is foundational to Grace.

Have we sought forgiveness for ourselves or asked forgiveness of ourselves?

Also means Accepting yourself for who God created you to be.

O – strife & situations become Opportunities for Love & Grace

1 John 3:16-20

We love God. He loves us. We love one another. Love heals. Love protects. God's Love and Peace transcend all human understanding. Love, coupled with God's peace, guards our hearts and minds with the power of Christ.

God wants each of us whole; for Him & in Him to be an integral part of His Plan

Homework: Meditate on and memorize 1 Corinthians 10:13 (in addition to the Philippians 4:6-9 above). Use these as “circuit breakers” for anxiety. Change what you listen to & read & watch. Remember GIGO. Garbage In, Garbage Out.

Finding Joy: Philippians, Regular Maintenance

Verses: Philippians 4:8-9; Galatians 5:22-25; Romans 1:18-32

Key Questions:

What needs maintenance in your life?

How do we transform our minds?

How do we produce Spiritual fruit?

The Noetic Effects of Sin:

Romans 1:18 – 32

Discuss the definition of "noetic" and why this is important to understand.

The Solution to Transforming our minds:

1. **True or Truth** – why is Truth listed first?
   John 3:33

2. **Honorable or Noble** – what are pictures of nobility?

3. **Right or Righteous** – other centered vs. self-centered
   self-sacrificial
   Ezra 9:15

4. **Pure** – lacks guile, no agenda or ulterior motive
   clean, nothing added
   Habakkuk 1:13

5. **Lovely** – pleasing to the senses
   brings about calmness & peace vs chaos & disorderliness
   Psalm 84:1

6. **Admirable** – something or someone to look up to
   ideas, certain people & their actions,
   ultimately Jesus
   Hebrews 12:1-2

7. Excellent – someone or something that has reached its zenith

excellence is a superlative
Psalm 45:1-2

8. Praiseworthy – as something is excellent, it should also be worthy of praise

the field of praiseworthy people or topics is narrow!
Jesus is truly the only One worthy of our praise
Philippians 2:10-11

The bottom line…

Jesus is the full embodiment of all of these "things to think on"

Jesus is the One that we should have on our minds at all times

Homework: Think about how we can change or modify our thoughts and thought processes to become more like Jesus and find true Joy in this earthly life.

Finding Joy: Philippians, Strong Enough

Verses: Philippians 4:10-20, Isaiah 40:28-31, Ephesian 3:14-19, 1 Corinthians 15:57-58

Key Questions:
What is God's way of doing things?
What does it mean to be "strong" and "satisfied"?

God's way of doing Life:

Isaiah 40:28-31

How are we satisfied?

What does it mean to be "satisfied" or "content"?

Being a student of life means that we must become a student of God:

1. Not my ease - 2 Corinthians 12:7-10

2. Not my riches - Ephesians 3:14-19

3. Not my victories - 1 Corinthians 15:57-58

4. Not my salvation - Isaiah 12:2-3, Job 19:25-27

5. Not my strength - Psalm 121

6. Not my plans – Jeremiah 29:11-13

7. Not my life – 1 Corinthians 6:20, 7:23

Homework: Look back at your life. Look at where you were in those hard times and contrast that to where God has brought you to today. Regularly making the time to reflect back is good as it provides the proper perspective we all need.

Weeping may tarry for the night, but joy comes with the morning. Psalm 30:5

Finding Joy: Philippians, Therefore…

Verses: Philippians

Key Question:

What is the "therefore" there for?

How does the Christian do life "better" than the non-Christian?

"Yets" & "Therefores":

1. Yet: Philippians 1:22

2. Therefore: Philippians 2:9-10

3. Therefore: Philippians 2:12-13

4. Therefore: Philippians 2:23

5. Therefore: Philippians 2:28

6. Therefore: Philippians 4:1

7. Yet: Philippians 4:14

Two Conclusions:

1. Christianity & the Bible are completely relevant to and for today's life & society.

2. There is no life worth living without God.

Homework (for the rest of your life): Understand at many times and circumstances, that life is hard. Find Joy! Look for beauty. Look for kindness. Look for the peace that only God can provide. When you find those things, you will find Joy. That's God's promise!

Discover A Deeper Walk... the series

From Doubt to Defense Each of us wants to share our faith, but most of us struggle to actually do. ***From Doubt to Defense*** is a bible study & workbook following the Book of Acts, examining stories and strategies from those first Christians that Jesus called and used to bring His Word and Salvation to the world.

Available in English & Spanish. For small group, Sunday school (teen to adult) or personal study.

Finding Power in Prayer Christians are called to pray. We pray for a variety of reasons, but often it feels like those words aren't going anywhere. ***Finding Power in Prayer*** is a Bible study that goes through the Scriptures, focusing on Daniel's prayer in chapter 9 as a great example of what our prayer life should look like and how God can better use His children to advance His Kingdom.

Available in English & Spanish. For small group, Sunday school (teen to adult) or personal study.

Finding Joy when Life is Hard. Yes, even when life seems to be beating us down, we can find Joy. Paul's epistle to the Philippians reminds us that we find joy in Jesus. ***Finding Joy when Life is Hard*** is a Bible study It doesn't mean that our lives will be trouble free, but we can find joy and contentment in the face of adversity and difficulty when we learn to cling to God's truths.

Available in English & Spanish. For small group, Sunday school (teen to adult) or personal study.

Coming soon!

Finding Strength in Grace. Grace is not weakness. Grace is both the motive and the motivator of how God operates in His universe and especially in our lives as He works out His Plan. ***Finding Strength in Grace*** is a study through God's Word that highlights the various attributes of Grace and how we should make them an integral part of our lives.

Available in English & Spanish. For small group, Sunday school (teen to adult) or personal study.

www.MyDeeperWalk.com

www.ingramcontent.com/pod-product-compliance
Lightning Source LLC
LaVergne TN
LVHW061203120826
845149LV00011B/1888
9798994747360